The Spread
of Civilization

Ron Carter

Macdonald/Silver Burdett

Editorial Manager	Chester Fisher
Senior Editor	Lynne Sabel
Editor	John Rowlstone
Assistant Editor	Bridget Daly
Series Designers	QED (Alastair Campbell and Edward Kinsey)
Designers	Jim Marks
	Nigel Osborne
Series Consultant	Keith Lye
Consultant	Peter Clayton
Production	Penny Kitchenham
Picture Research	Jenny de Gex

© Macdonald Educational Ltd. 1978
First published 1978
Reprinted 1979
Macdonald Educational Ltd.
Holywell House
Worship Street
London EC2A 2EN

Published in the
United States by
Silver Burdett Company
Morristown, N.J.
1980 Printing
ISBN 0-382-06408-9

World of Knowledge

This book breaks new ground in the method it uses to present information to the reader. The unique page design combines narrative with an alphabetical reference section and it uses colourful photographs, diagrams and illustrations to provide an instant and detailed understanding of the book's theme. The main body of information is presented in a series of chapters that cover, in depth, the subject of this book. At the bottom of each page is a reference section which gives, in alphabetical order, concise articles which define, or enlarge on, the topics discussed in the chapter. Throughout the book, the use of SMALL CAPITALS in the text directs the reader to further information that is printed in the reference section. The same method is used to cross-reference entries within each reference section. Finally, there is a comprehensive index at the end of the book that will help the reader find information in the text, illustrations and reference sections. The quality of the text, and the originality of its presentation, ensure that this book can be read both for enjoyment and for the most up-to-date information on the subject.

Contents

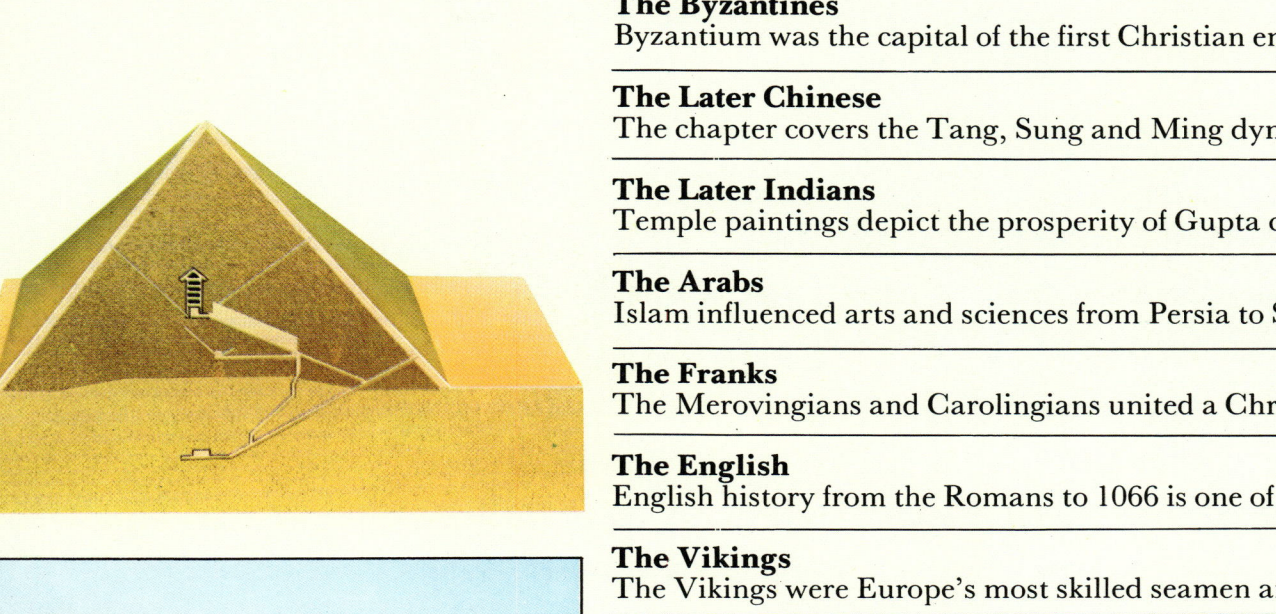

The Greeks Greek culture formed the cornerstone of western civilization.	3
The Etruscans Etruria had a distinctive culture based on city-states.	10
The Celts The Celts were a warrior race originating from Central Europe.	12
The Macedonians The short life of Alexander is a dramatic adventure story.	14
The Romans At its height the Roman empire covered over 6 million square kilometres. Their road network is still in use today.	17
The Byzantines Byzantium was the capital of the first Christian empire.	24
The Later Chinese The chapter covers the Tang, Sung and Ming dynasties.	26
The Later Indians Temple paintings depict the prosperity of Gupta court life.	30
The Arabs Islam influenced arts and sciences from Persia to Spain.	33
The Franks The Merovingians and Carolingians united a Christian Europe.	40
The English English history from the Romans to 1066 is one of invasion.	42
The Vikings The Vikings were Europe's most skilled seamen and explorers.	44
The Feudal Europeans Feudalism provided the basis for the Renaissance in Europe.	46
The Africans The ancient cultures south of the Sahara traded in gold.	49
The Japanese The unique character of Japan evolved through its isolation.	52
The Mongols The nomadic armies of Genghiz Khan swept across Asia.	54
The Central Americans These peoples included the Maya, Olmecs and Zapotecs.	56
The Aztecs This tribe was obsessed with human sacrifice to the gods.	59
The Incas Inca society was organized as a kind of welfare state.	62
Index	65

Introduction

The Spread of Civilization covers world history from the height of Greek culture and 'the glory that was Rome' to around the start of the Age of Exploration in the 1400s. It shows how indebted Europeans are to Greece and Rome but, after the fall of Rome, the focus of world history often shifts away from Europe and **The Spread of Civilization** sheds light on important developments elsewhere. For example, during Europe's so-called 'Dark Ages', it was the Arabs of the Middle East and North Africa who preserved classical learning and it was Arab scholarship which provided much of the inspiration for the European explorers of the 1400s. By taking a global view, we can better appreciate the inter-action between human cultures and understand the shifting patterns of greatness and decadence, achieving a balanced view of man's constant quest for knowledge and progress.

The culture of the ancient Greeks forms the cornerstone of Western civilization. In philosophy and art the Greeks remain largely unsurpassed to this day. Even in science and medicine they led the field until modern times.

The Greeks

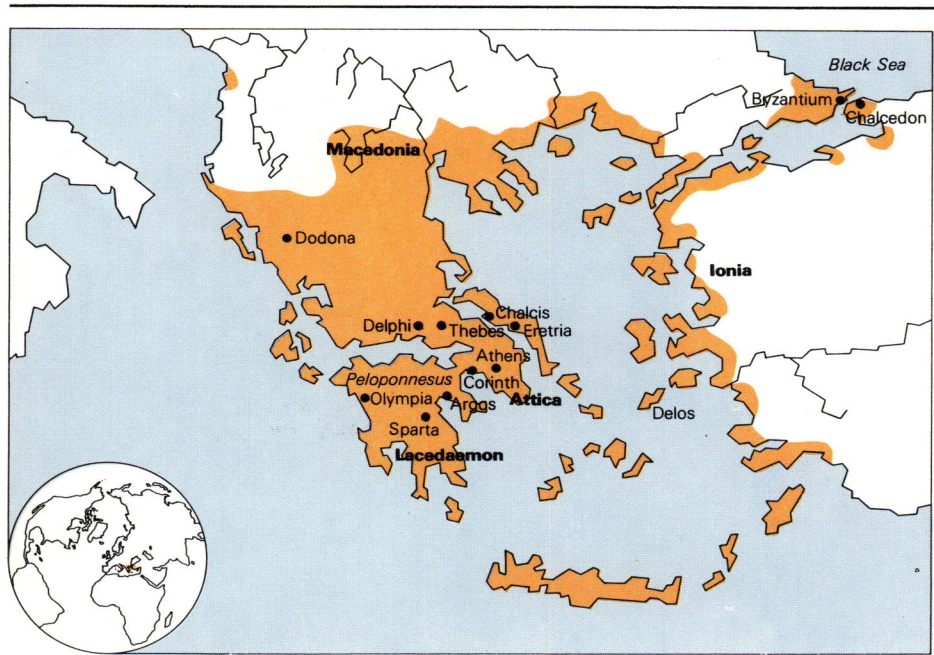

Above: Cities in the craggy peninsula of ancient Greece seldom stood far from the sea, which heavily influenced Greek history. Greeks early on founded colonies along the coastlands of Asia Minor, then spread throughout the Mediterranean and Black Seas.

Right: The head of Pericles wearing his warrior's helmet symbolizes the great age of Athenian democracy which he established in 462–454 BC. Under Pericles all citizens became eligible to hold the highest government posts, but citizenship was limited to men having both parents of Athenian birth.

The Greek civilization was a small one compared with the empires of the Persians, Chinese and Indians, occupying the southern part of present-day Greece, an area no larger than Sri Lanka or a single Persian satrapy (province). Only 25 per cent of this territory could be cultivated and so even at the height of its civilization Greece never exceeded a population of two millions, barely 10 per cent that of Chou China during the same period. The lives of the people of the Greek city-states were dominated by the surrounding sea and the Greeks became enterprising colonists although they never founded empires.

Greek achievements

Greek culture forms the basis of our present-day western civilization and was centred on Athens, which was already in political decline when at its cultural height in the 400s BC. The Greeks were great experimenters and innovators in many areas such as government, philosophy and architecture, and many consider that in the arts, and more especially in sculpture, they remain largely unsurpassed to this day. Their theories in science and medicine, though often wrong were accepted by western Europe until only a few hundred years ago. Many western European languages owe the origin of their vocabularies to the Greek language; western drama had its beginnings in Greek theatre; and Greek mythology has left the West a treasure trove of stories still told today. As for sports, every leap year the world commemorates the Olympic Games held in Greece for over 1,000 years.

Despite their advanced culture, the Greeks were in some ways as barbarian as any other ancient people. Their civilization was founded on a slave society and women were no more highly regarded than they were by any of their contemporary societies. Surplus girl children and weaklings unlikely to be able to survive unsup-

Reference

Acropolis was the fortified hill of a Greek city which often contained the main temple and other sacred buildings. The most famous acropolis is that of Athens, on which the PARTHENON stands.

Aeschylus (525–456 BC) wrote about 80 plays in which he analyzed the relationship between man and God in history. Only 7 survive, including *Agamemnon* (part of a trilogy). His plays always involved 2 actors, whereas earlier plays had used only 1.

Amphorae are egg-shaped, 2-handled jars with narrow necks and there are 2 distinct kinds. Plain ones held corn, honey, oil or wine and usually had pointed bases for lodging in the earth. Decorated amphorae were given as prizes in games and the government of Athens encouraged their production in 'cottage industries' to promote export.

Apollo, god of light and purity, was the son of Zeus. He was believed to reveal the future to people through his oracles at Delphi. Supposedly skilled in poetry, music, archery and medicine, Apollo was re-

Amphora: Ajax and Achilles

garded as the ideal of manly beauty.

Architecture in Greece from the 600s BC onwards is called *classical* and had 3 orders set by the style of the fluted columns. *Doric* columns were the oldest and simplest; *Ionic* columns were more slender, graceful and decorated, and *Corinthian* columns, variations on the Ionic, were even more ornamental. These orders and their variations are still used by architects.

Aristophanes (c.445–c.385 BC) wrote 44 comedies, 11 of which survive. The most noted of these are *Lysistrata* and the *Frogs*. He satirized people, institutions and events of his times with a penetrating shrewdness and

Temple of Athena Nike

4 The Greeks

Right: The temple of Athena at Delphi, built about 320 BC, stood near the site of the oracle where a priestess answered crucial questions. Her pronouncements were often ambiguous, as when she said: 'If Croesus should make war on the Persians he would destroy a mighty empire.'

Below: The three main Greek orders of columns show an increase in elegance and decoration from the earliest Doric to the Corinthian.

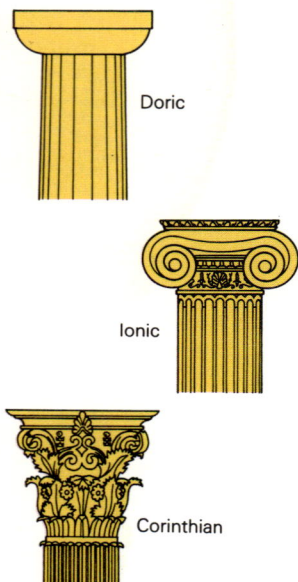

ported were taken to the waste lands to die of exposure. Greek city-states were more often at war with each other than in alliance, and it was their compulsive rivalry and greed that eventually brought about the downfall of the Greek civilization.

Government, philosophy and law

About 1000 BC groups of Greek-speaking invaders, the Dorians, began pouring into Greece from the Balkans and they ruled the city-states until about 600 BC. They brought with them iron weapons, tools and implements, the advent of which resulted in greater food production and a consequent rise in population. Dorian nobles kept the best land for themselves, sustained an autocracy, and dispensed justice as they thought fit. But as population outgrew food supply, emigration increased and rebellions broke out in several states replacing the Dorians by popular leaders. The Greeks called these popular leaders tyrants (meaning 'lords'), but they soon became as self-seeking as the old rulers and the word tyrant came to mean 'oppressor'. In the 500s BC there was a new wave of rebellions and states toppled their tyrants and found new rulers.

The new governments formed differed throughout the city-states. Attica (of which Athens was the capital) set up a limited DEMOCRACY and Corinth came to be governed by an OLIGARCHY (government of leading families). SPARTA remained unchanged, and was still ruled by a military caste of Dorians who imposed an iron discipline on their subjects. Their harsh, comfortless way of life has given us our present-day meaning of the word 'spartan'.

About 450–320 BC Greece was a melting pot for ideas on government and all other aspects of life. Philosophers and schools of philosophy became fashionable. One of the most famous was run by

---

the underlying truth of his humorous criticism is as relevant today as it was in ancient Greece.
Aristotle (384–322 BC) was one of the greatest thinkers of all time, but he differed on several matters with his tutor, PLATO. Aristotle had more interest in law and science, and created the thought system of logic. His theories on astronomy, the nature of the atom and the origins of life, were slavishly followed into medieval times in Europe, and only much later did scientists prove them wrong.

Autocracy is rule by an autocrat, one who rules by his own power and without reference to others.

Aristotle

B **Byzantium,** founded by the city-state of Megara in 667 BC, later came under Roman rule. It became the capital of the Byzantine empire.

C **Citizenship** in Athens was restricted to those having 2 Athenian parents from 451 BC.
Cynics were philosophers in the 300s BC who believed that virtue was better than pleasure, wealth or honours. Their school was founded by Antisthenes, a disciple of SOCRATES. Diogenes was an example of an extreme cynic who ate the coarsest bread and slept in a tub. The word cynic has come to mean one who has little faith in human goodness.

D **Delian League** was a naval alliance which Athens made to her great advantage with many Ionian states who were not always allied with each other. Athens decided how many ships or how much money each state should contribute. Her own contribution was 200 triremes. In the allied attack on the Persians in 466 BC, the Athenian ships carried 5,000 hoplites and were supported by 100 Ionian ships carrying marines and archers. Under PERICLES, Athens came to treat the

Demeter

Right: Theatrical masks were first used by Greek actors, who took the idea from religious practices. On the stage, masks became complex headpieces made of leather or painted canvas. Comic masks were often grotesque, having grimacing mouths and beards.

Right: Odysseus (Ulysses), one of the great heroes of Homer's works, became incorporated into the Greek mythology. Determined not to succumb to the sirens whose singing lured sailors to their doom on a barren island, Odysseus plugged the ears of his seamen. His men then bound him so that he could listen in safety.

Above: Greek theatres were considered the most remarkable of their time for their symmetry and beauty, but also for their striking acoustics. Even a whisper from the round orchestra or the stage could be heard by the seated audience.

SOCRATES, an open-air teacher who taught by question and answer, and wrote nothing. PLATO was one of his pupils, and the author of the *Republic,* which examined the place of the just man in the ideal society. This work is still studied today. In his turn, Plato tutored ARISTOTLE, who wrote *Politics,* a more scientific study of government, and was the teacher of the boy destined to become Alexander the Great.

Apart from these outstanding figures, there were two groups of philosophers: the CYNICS, who strove for virtue rather than learning and pleasure; and STOICS, who recommended men to follow pure reason free from passion.

The law of Athens was unwritten until DRACO set down a code in 621 BC. Some of his punishments were so severe that the word 'draconian' has come to mean excessively harsh. The laws of SOLON, an Athenian lawgiver, were more enlightened, as he laid down a single code for rich and poor alike. By giving votes to all those who had CITIZENSHIP, Solon also laid the basis of Athenian democracy, which enjoyed a 'golden age' about 458–445 BC under the leadership of PERICLES.

Greek religion and mythology

GREEK RELIGION, like Hindu, developed over the ages and involved the worship of deities who had the forms and characters of humans. The first wave of Aryan Greeks brought deities like Zeus, Poseidon, APOLLO, DEMETER and HERMES and later absorbed Mycenaean and Cretan deities.

The Greeks had no sacred books such as the *Avesta*, Bible, *Vedas* or *Suttas*. Instead they had works of literature by poets such as Homer and HESIOD which portrayed the deities in human situations. Most Greeks believed in pacifying their deities with prayers and sacrifices and asking their advice by consulting ORACLES.

Arts and language

Greek architecture pioneered a new style, the outstanding examples of which were the PARTHENON and other buildings set on the ACROPOLIS at Athens. Unlike the Babylonians, the Greeks did not use the arch in their architecture and Greek sculpture centred especially on the quest for perfection in the human form, which was often portrayed naked. Greek artists also developed a lively two-dimensional art, much of which has survived on vases and AMPHORAE.

Greek playwrights were the first to present drama in the modern sense. ARISTOPHANES wrote comedies; AESCHYLUS, SOPHOCLES and EURIPIDES produced tragedies; poetry continued in the high standard set by Homer, and HERODOTUS, THUCYDIDES and XENOPHON wrote histories. It was an age of great orators. Isocrates set up a school of oratory and rhetoric to rival Plato's Academy and Demosthenes spoke vigorously against

---

Ionian states as colonies rather than allies.

Demeter was goddess of corn and agriculture.

Democracy is rule by the whole people, although some of the people are always excluded (for example, children). Athenian democracy excluded slaves, women and metics. Direct democracy, in which people actually vote for or against policies, could be possible only in the small city-state. Large modern states are only democracies in the sense that people elect representatives.

Draco introduced the first written code of laws in Athens in 621 BC. It sought to end blood feuds between families and satisfy people who wanted to be answerable to a written code rather than be subject to the whims of aristocratic judges.

E Euripides (480–406 BC) wrote over 90 short plays, each about 1,500 lines of blank verse. Only 19 have survived, including the *Bacchae* and *Trojan Women*. Euripides tackled political, ethical and psychological problems recognizable in our own times. His works include myths about the deities updated to suit the temper of his own times.

Euripedes

G Greek civilization was the parent of the present western civilization. It holds a special interest for western people because most aspects of Greek culture can be linked to present-day society; even the psychology of the West is nearer to Greece than to other early civilizations.

Greek religion taught that the universe was a sphere. The upper half was said to have light and fresh air; the lower half to be dark and dank. The earth was believed to be a flat disc midway between the 2 halves which floated on the waters of the underworld. Deities, it was believed, came after, and not before, creation. Each city-state had its special deity, such as Athena, goddess of Athens, who competed for the position against Poseidon, and won.

H Hermes was the herald-god of his father, Zeus, and sometimes escorted people to Hades. He was also god of peaceful commerce, prudence, cunning, theft, weights and measures, astronomy, olive culture,

6 The Greeks

Above: The Parthenon, built on the acropolis of Athens in honour of the goddess Athena, still dominates the city. It is a supreme example of the Doric style of architecture.

boxing and gymnastics. He wore a traveller's hat, wings, and winged sandles.

Herodotus (c.484–c.424 BC), called the 'father of history', wrote the history of the world up to his own time. His anecdotal accounts are highly entertaining but sometimes of doubtful accuracy. He travelled widely in the eastern Mediterranean in search of material for his writings, studying people and places.

Hesiod (700s BC) was the first great Greek poet after Homer. His *Works and Days* gave instructions on farming and advice on work to be done on specific days. It also contained the story of *Pandora's Box*. (Pandora, the first woman, disobeyed the gods by opening her gift box, so releasing all the troubles that have since plagued mankind.) In his *Theogony* Hesiod tried to reconcile conflicting stories about the deities.

Hoplites were heavily armed soldiers whose function was to fight in close formation. Their introduction marked a basic change in tactical warfare and the decline of chariots and cavalry. They wore metal helmets, breast-plates, *greaves* (armour below the knees), and shields, and carried spears and swords. The hoplite phalanx (*see* INFANTRY

Hoplites

page 15) was normally 8 ranks deep. Greek hoplites were valued abroad as mercenaries, while at home, their power strengthened the middle class and speeded the end of the old aristocracy.

Mathematics was advanced considerably by the work of Greek mathematicians and philosophers, who favoured it for its theoretical rather than practical nature. Pythagoras (c.580-500 BC) studied numbers and especially geometry. He discovered that in a right-angled triangle, the square of the hypotenuse is equal to the sum of the squares of the other two sides. Euclid (300s BC), the 'father of geometry', wrote *The Elements,* a series of 13 books still used as the basis of geometry. Archimedes (c.287-212 BC), who discovered formulae for curves, spheres and spirals, was among the greatest mathematicians of all time. He probably invented the Archimedean screw, a device to draw water.

Medicine was pioneered by Hippocrates of Cos (469-399

Philip II of Macedonia.

The ancient Greek language was related to Hittite, although its present alphabet, founded about 1000 BC, derived from the Phoenician. Being isolated from one another, the Greek city-states spoke different dialects, but Attic, spoken in Athens, came to be the most important language of Greek literature. From 300 BC, Greek became the international language of cultured people.

Social structure

The class structure of ancient Greece varied from state to state. In Attica, citizens were the most numerous class, followed by slaves and *metics* (resident foreigners). In Lacedaemon (of which Sparta was the capital), *helots* (serfs) formed the largest class, followed by Spartiates (citizens descended from Dorians), and *perioeci* (non-citizens). Slaves usually belonged to private owners, but some governments used them as miners. Serfs could own personal property, but could not leave their place of birth. Metics and *perioeci* had freedom, but neither they nor any women had political rights.

Athenian citizens

Solon established four classes of citizens in Attica, based on the wealth of the land they farmed. The top class (*pentacosiomedimnoi*) were those who produced at least 750 bushels of wheat or 20,000 litres of wine or oil a year. The next class (known as *horsemen*) were those whose land provided 60 per cent of that amount. The third rank of citizens (known as HOPLITES) had to produce 40 per cent of the product of the top class. All citizens below this level of production were *thetes* (day labourers). As their names suggest, the second and third classes became cavalry soldiers and infantry (hoplites) in war time, while the poverty-stricken *thetes* probably handled an oar on the triremes during naval battles.

All adult male citizens, of whom there may have been 80,000, could vote in the Assembly, sit as jurors, and become candidates for certain offices according to rank. Travel to the Assembly was not difficult, because the whole of Attica was smaller than Greater London – or half the size of Rhode Island. But poorer men often declined to attend because even after payment for public service was introduced, they could not afford to leave their farms.

Metics and slaves in Attica

Metics were traders not from choice, but because, as foreigners, they were not permitted to own land. Nevertheless, they seldom grew rich because Attica was a poor state with few exports, apart from the occasional surplus of olives or some other crop. Exports might also have included the products of the potters who were set to work by the state to produce luxury vases and amphorae for trade purposes.

Industry did not exist on a large scale, and the largest workshop probably belonged to Cephalus, a metic from Syracuse, who kept 120 slaves making shields. Few others employed more than 20 or 30. Slaves were used to non-agricultural manual work, but most of the 80,000 of them in Greece worked on farms or as domestic servants. According to the comedies of Aristophanes, they seem to have been given rough treatment and regular beatings by their owners.

Daily life in Greece

Most Greeks lived simply in town houses built of stone or sun-dried brick, whose windowless walls backed onto narrow alleyways. Each room had a

Above: The picture on the amphora shows workers knocking down olives from a tree. Olives and other fruit were sold in the *agora*. Amphorae were often produced in state workshops in Athens as part of 'job creation schemes' to provide employment.

Left: The temple of Hephaestus, set on the hill Colonus Agoraeus, dominated the *agora* (market place) of Athens. In the foreground, a trader offers 2 fair-skinned slaves for sale. Earthen vessels, sandals, fish and other goods are laid out for sale to the left. 2 scholars, members perhaps of one of the many schools in the city, enjoy an argument to the right. The agora provided a general meeting place for the Athenians.

BC), who set up medical schools in Athens and elsewhere. He tried to separate medicine from superstition. Hippocrates is called the 'father of medicine' but it is probable that he borrowed heavily from the *Ayurvedic* system of medicine laid down in the sacred Hindu *Vedas*. Greek doctors were respected in the ancient world. They were less superstitious than Roman doctors.

O **Oligarchy** is rule by a small exclusive class – sometimes a group of families or a caste.

Olympic Games were held at Olympia in honour of Zeus. In addition to sports, they included competitions in art, drama, gymnastics, literature, music and rhetoric. They continued (with intervals) from 776 BC to AD 394 and were reintroduced in 1896.

Oracles were supposed responses by deities to questions put to them. Usually they were uttered by priests or priestesses, who were also called oracles. Leading oracles were those of Zeus at Dodona and Apollo at Delphi.

P **Parthenon,** the temple sacred to Athena, was built 444-432 BC under PERICLES and is often considered to be the greatest achievement of Greek architecture. Its architects were Ictinus and Callicrates, and Phidias supervised the sculptures.

Apollo and Artemis

Peloponnesian League, or Spartan Alliance, was formed about 550 BC. States adjoining Sparta received its protection, in return agreeing to serve under Spartan command in war, and to assist Sparta against possible risings of the helots. By 510 BC, almost all the Peloponnesian states except Argos had joined. The League fought the first Peloponnesian war against the Athenian-led DELIAN LEAGUE in 460–445 BC, and the second Peloponnesian war in 431–404 BC.

Pericles (c.490–429 BC), an aristocrat, was the champion

Plato

8 The Greeks

Below: Hoplites, the heavily armoured infantrymen of ancient Greece, fought in close formation. They came from the middle class. Their military success ended the dominance of the cavalry and chariots in war, and of the old feudal aristocracy in society. Greek hoplites fought with thrusting spears instead of the throwing spears of earlier soldiers. Hoplite phalanxes smashed through enemy ranks to throw the line into disorder.

door leading to an inner courtyard and country houses, farms and yards were enclosed by stone walls. Charcoal was burned to give warmth in the cold winters.

Most people ate two meals a day. The mid-morning meal might be a bowl of peas or beans with a raw onion or cooked turnip, while evening meals often included bread, cheese, olives, figs and occasionally meat or fish. Honey sweetened the food, and olive oil was used for cooking as well as a kind of soap. The Greeks drank either water or wine. Milk, they thought, was only for 'barbarians' (all non-Greeks).

Men and women alike wore a *chiton* – a gown that dropped to the knees or ankles. Chitons were commonly of wool, but rich people had them made of cotton or linen. Cloaks or capes were worn as overgarments.

Colonization

There were two great colonizing nations in the ancient world: the Greeks and the Phoenicians, who were the first to colonize on a major scale. (They founded Carthage 80 years before the Greeks did Syracuse in 734 BC, although by the 300s BC Syracuse had outstripped Corinth in population and then numbered 250,000 inhabitants.) The two major powers shared Cyprus amicably, but clashed during the 500s BC in Sicily.

Beginning about 750 BC, groups of landless Greek peasants set sail from mainland and island ports. Those from the Ionian states of Chalcis and Eretria founded colonies at Cumae and Aenaria in western Italy, and in Sicily; Spartans settled at Tarentum in southern Italy; Corinth founded Syracuse in Sicily; Megara colonized BYZANTIUM and Chalcedon, and Thera established Cyrene. More colonies were planted along the coasts of present-day Spain, France, Corsica, Sardinia, Yugoslavia and Egypt.

While Greek colonists appeared to have no ambitions to found empires, they sought, and usually gained, the co-operation of the peoples of the lands in which they settled. Colonization was accompanied by a strengthening of Greek sea power and the harbours of overseas settlements were soon bustling with the activities of Greek trading ships. Trading opportunities encouraged further emigration and the Greeks of Asia Minor colonized the coastlands of the Black Sea.

of Athenian democracy. He dominated Athens 460–430 BC, a period known as the 'Age of Pericles'. He fought a series of naval wars against Persia and Sparta and died of the plague when Athens, her power broken by war, finally submitted to Sparta.
Philosophy flourished in Greece 450–320 BC. The great philosophers made original contributions to human thought, although their subject matter had little to do directly with the serious problems of their times. To some extent, the intellectual concerns of the philosophers were a form of escape from reality, and the Athenian philosophers were at their most eloquent when Athens was dying because of its political errors.
Plato (c.427–c.347 BC), pupil of SOCRATES and tutor of ARISTOTLE, founded the Academy to teach philosophy and mathematics. He presented much of his writings in the form of conversations and letters, and the *Republic* was his greatest work.

Science in Greece was pursued for intellectual rather than practical purposes, and few scientists actually put their theories to the test. Early Greek philosophers who concerned themselves with scientific matters included Thales (624–565 BC); Anaximander (611–547 BC); and Anaximenes (570–? BC). Democritus (c.470–400 BC) came uncannily close to the truth in his theory of atomic energy, and ARISTOTLE propounded theories on astronomy, atomic structure and the nature of life which, though misguided, were accepted until modern times.

Socrates (469–399 BC) concerned himself with the right choice between good and bad. Goodness, he believed, stemmed from wisdom;

Socrates

badness from ignorance. He encouraged discussion about all aspects of human relationships and taught by question and answer. Socrates thought nothing should be exempted from intellectual scrutiny. The Athenian government convicted him of heresy and corruption of youth. He was condemned to death and died by drinking hemlock in prison.
Solon (c.638–c.559 BC), an Athenian lawgiver, cancelled debts owed by the farmers of Attica. He freed those enslaved for debt and estab-

The Persian and first Peloponnesian war

Under the Persian empire, the Greeks of Asia Minor could run their own affairs so long as they did not oppose Persian interests. When the Ionian city-states revolted against Persia in 499 BC, they had at least the moral support of their fellow Greeks in mainland Greece. Although Sparta refused direct aid, Athens sent the Ionians 20 ships and Eretria sent five. So began the Greco-Persian wars which ended in Greek victory over the Persians and their Phoenician mercenary fleets at Salamis (480 BC) and at Plataea and Mycale (479 BC).

Although the Persians lost, the Greeks expected them to strike again. Sparta feared that Ionia could not be held, and advised the Greeks there to emigrate, while Athens held that Ionia could be defended by sea – especially if the Athenian fleet kept the Phoenicians out of the Aegean. In fact both states had ulterior motives for their advice. Sparta feared that its helots would revolt if its army went overseas and Athens saw the chance to increase its own influence.

In 478–477 BC Athens, with several small Ionian city-states, entered into a naval alliance known as the DELIAN LEAGUE. Athens and its 200 triremes took the command in battle and received half of all the booty won. The Athenians also became custodians of the Delian League's funds which were kept at Delos, an island between Greece and Asia Minor. The Delian League successfully attacked the Persians in Europe and in Asia Minor, which led their Spartan rivals to suspect them of planning to create a Greek empire.

Flushed with success, Athens led the allied navy into a war on two fronts in 460 BC. It defeated the navy of the Spartan-led PELOPONNESIAN LEAGUE, then sailed up the Nile and laid siege to the Persian garrisons in Egypt. But the Persians cleverly diverted the waters of the Nile, trapped and captured one Athenian-led navy, and destroyed another sent to relieve it. Its naval power temporarily crippled, Athens prudently sought a truce with Sparta. This was granted only in 445 BC, after five years of negotiation.

The second Peloponnesian war

In 431 BC, following Athenian provocation, Sparta led Corinth and other states of the Peloponnesian League into war against the Delian League. Athens, with its port of Piraeus, stood secure behind its walls, but the Spartans reduced the surrounding territory to wasteland and then a plague broke out in the city, claiming Pericles as one of its victims. Plague and war killed off over 30 per cent of the Athenian population. Several of Athens' allies defected, and some joined Sparta. Civil wars, guerrilla warfare, atrocities and disease carried misery throughout all Greece.

Peace came in 421 BC, but only briefly, as the war resumed in 413 BC when Sparta gained Persian aid at the price of abandoning the Greek settlements in Asia Minor. Eventually, in 406 BC Lysander, the Spartan admiral, defeated the Athenians and starved them into submission. From 404 BC Sparta led Greece, but its severe rule brought rebellion. In 371 BC, Thebes defeated Sparta and took the leadership. Exhausted and leaderless, Greece slipped into anarchy. Finally in 338 BC, Philip II of Macedon crushed a last desperate alliance of Greek states. Soon after this the whole of European Greece was absorbed into the Macedonian empire.

Above: These 2 coins show the front of a Hellenistic galley c.300 BC (*above*) and the front of a Carthaginian galley c.200 BC (*below*).

Below: Surrounded by the sea, the Greeks rivalled the Phoenicians as traders and outdid them as colonists. Greek warships were either *biremes* having 2 banks of oars (like the one shown) or *triremes* with 3 banks of oars.

---

lished 4 classes of citizens.
Sophocles (496–406 BC) wrote over 100 plays, mostly tragedies, only 7 of which including *Antigone*, *Electra* and *Oedipus Rex*, survive. His themes included relationships between man and the city-state, and the struggle of strong individuals against fate. His characters are more down-to-earth than those in AESCHYLUS. Sophocles introduced a third actor and fixed the chorus at 15.
Sparta was the capital of Lacedaemon (or Laconia), to which it has given its name. It was perhaps the most completely military state in history. True Spartans scorned easy living and accepted harsh discipline. Strong abroad, Sparta was

Spartan soldier

vulnerable at home: 25,000 *Spartiates* (Dorian-descended citizens) held as many as 50,000 helots in serfdom, and the helots often rebelled when the Spartan army went away to war. Spartan boys trained for war from the age of 7 and book learning was considered unnecessary. A Spartan finally retired from the army – if he lived – at 60. Spartan women had more freedom than other Greek women.
Stoics (300s BC) believed that the proper use of knowledge was to help men find their proper place in nature. No matter what good or evil befell a man, he should remain calm and unruffled. If a stoic thought he had control over a situation he should do as he wished. If not, there was no point in trying to alter the situation. Nowadays, we would say that he accepted the position 'stoically'.

T **Thucydides** (c.460–c.400 BC), an Athenian naval commander, wrote the precise but unfinished *History of the Peloponnesian War*, from which most of our information on this period comes.

X **Xenophon** (c.430–c.355 BC), a Greek mercenary soldier, became commander of 10,000 Greek mercenaries stranded in Persia. He wrote the history of their retreat.

The Etruscans are set in history between the great cultures of the Greeks and the Romans. They learned much from the former and passed on much to the latter, yet their civilization was unique.

The Etruscans

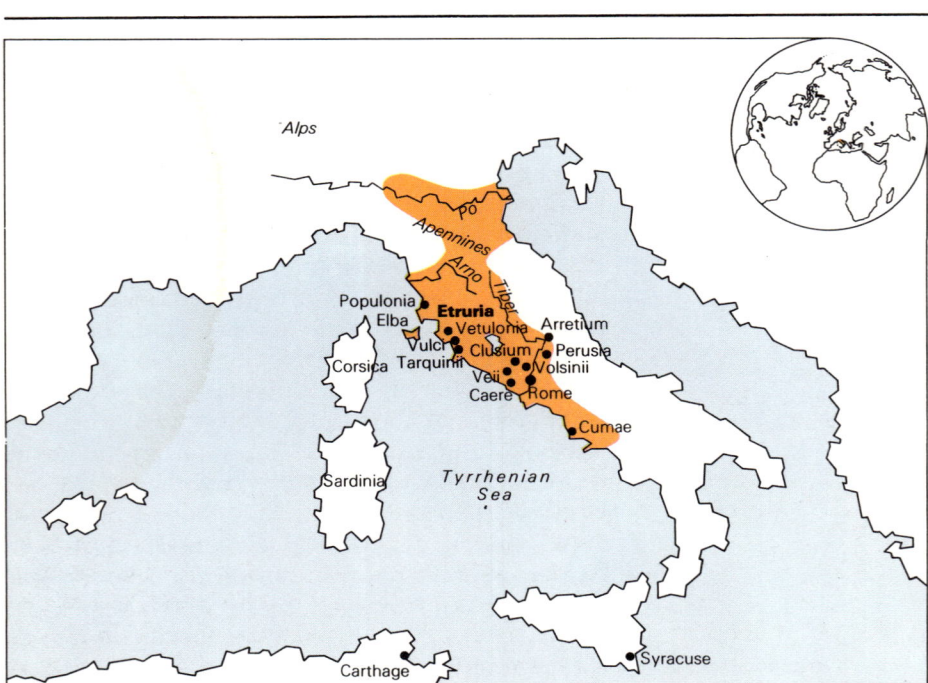

Above: The city states of Etruria occupied roughly the area of modern Tuscany southwards to Rome, but the Etruscan frontiers later extended to the Po Valley.

Left: An Etruscan couple recline together in a manner suggesting equality of status between them – a concept rarely found in the ancient world. The clay sculpture forms part of a sarcophagus dating from the 500s BC.

The Etruscan civilization flourished from about the 700s BC to the 200s BC and formed the basis for the later civilization of the Romans. It began in Etruria, the region of Italy now known as Tuscany, and extended northwards from the Tiber River to the Arno and later to the valley of the Po, and eastwards from the TYRRHENIAN SEA to the Apennine Mountains. No one knows for sure where the ETRUSCANS came from. Quite possibly they always lived in Italy, though Herodotus thought that they migrated from Lydia in the 1200s BC at about the time of the Trojan war.

Social structure

The Etruscans developed TWELVE CITY-STATES, each of which was governed by an aristocratic ruling caste formed of either priest-kings or magistrates. Cultural bonds linked the city-states, and although they had no permanent political union or military alliance, their representatives met annually at the sanctuary of the god VOLTUMNA, where they discussed religious, political and military matters.

A closely knit family system, where women had a great deal of freedom and near equality with men, formed the basis of Etruscan society. Between the nobles at the top of the social scale and the slaves at the bottom were freemen and probably a class of serfs, who worked as farm labourers, cooks, actors, musicians and dancers. From funerary inscriptions we know that the average life span was about 40 years. On average, Etruscan men were only 1.64 metres tall and Etruscan women, 1.55 metres.

Religion, arts and language

The Etruscans believed that the DEITIES who governed the universe had set rules for human conduct and decided in advance the destiny of Etruria. They were greatly concerned with life

Reference

C Celts were an Aryan warrior race who appeared in south-western Germany about 500 BC. Armed with iron weapons they swept on throughout western Europe, and for hundreds of years clashed with the Romans, who finally conquered them.
Colonies were established by the Etruscans in the Balearic Islands, Corsica, Elba, Sardinia and mainland Spain.

D Deities of the Etruscans can be equated with those of the Greeks, notably Tin (Zeus), Nethunes (Poseidon), and Apula (Apollo).

E Engineering projects carried out by the Etruscans included roadbuilding, hydraulic engineering, and the construction of aqueducts, bridges and sewers. They passed these skills on to the Romans.
Etruscans, claimed by Herodotus to have come from an area in ancient Asia Minor called Lydia, were said by later scholars to have been native to Italy, or to have migrated from north of the Alps. A history of the Etruscans was written by the Roman Emperor CLAUDIUS (see page 18).

Side panel of an urn

G Gauls were Celts who occupied present-day France, Belgium, and parts of Germany, Switzerland and the Netherlands.

H Haruspicy was the examination by *haruspices* (soothsayers or tellers of future events) of certain organs of sacrificial animals, especially the liver. It also included the interpretation of natural phenomena such as thunder, the pattern of lightning, the flights of birds, and the behaviour of animals. Haruspices worked according to rules laid down in sacred writings and had to be learned in science and technology.
Human figures were often elongated by Etruscan artists. During the present century, the Italian sculptor, Alberto Giacometti (1901–66) carried this Etruscan art mode to greater extremes.

M Marius, a poor-born Roman political general, fought a civil war against his opponent, SULLA. Etruria allied itself with Marius, but

after death and practised HARUSPICY to find out what had been decreed.

The art of the Etruscans was based on that of the Greeks, but they developed one unique feature: their HUMAN FIGURES were elongated and thinned, portrayed in lively movement and often with smiles or other recognizable expressions on their faces. These figures adorned tomb frescoes showing how the dead had enjoyed themselves during their lifetimes. Death was the major preoccupation of Etruscan artists and they cut elaborate funerary memorials from stone or volcanic lava and embellished them with bronze or clay effigies of their dead. In architecture, they used the arch, the dome and the vault long before the Romans.

The Etruscan alphabet was of Greek origin and the sounds of its letters are known, although its vocabulary has been lost. Most of its surviving writings deal with funerary practices.

Economic and social life

The Etruscans excelled at ENGINEERING, and there was plenty of scope to exercise their talent

Right: The tomb of a wealthy Etruscan, carved from solid rock to represent a room, had bed niches in the wall. Representations of armour, weapons and tools carved on the walls were intended to aid and protect the dead person in the next world.

Below: Two Etruscan soldiers carrying a fallen comrade stand immortalized in bronze. Etruscan bronzesmiths gained a reputation as masters of their craft.

because Etruria was rich in metals, especially iron. Metalworking, along with piracy, provided the main base of Etruscan wealth. Their exports included their goldwork which was among the best in the ancient world, and black bucchero pottery, for which they were renowned.

The rise and fall of Etruria

By the 700s BC Etruria had evolved a distinctive culture centred on its main city-states, TARQUINII, VEII and Perusia (now Perugia). In its prime Etruria was very powerful at sea and established many COLONIES, while on the mainland, in about 600 BC, the Etruscans founded Rome. When the Greeks barred their advance further southwards, the Etruscans allied themselves with the Carthaginians about 535 BC. But as it turned out, this was not a profitable move, because the terms of the alliance restricted their trade, and hastened their end as a sea power.

In 509 BC the Romans rebelled against the harsh rule of the Etruscan King Tarquinius Superbus the Proud, and declared an independent republic. This blow was followed by the crippling defeat of the Etruscan fleet by the Syracusans off Cumae in 474 BC and the fall of northern Etruria to the CELTS (whom the Romans called GAULS).

The rising power of Rome was gradually encroaching on Etruria, and the Etruscans lost Veii to the Romans about 396 BC. Civil war followed between the Etruscan city-states when some of them allied themselves with the Roman commander MARIUS against his rival, SULLA. When Sulla came to power in Rome in 86 BC, he swept away the last remnants of Etruscan independence and incorporated the city-states into the territory of Rome.

Sulla was the eventual victor.

Sulla (138–78 BC), a political general and aristocrat, finally triumphed in Rome on the death of his rival MARIUS, leader of the popular party. After his success he annexed Etruria, which had been allied to Marius.

Tarquinii. An Etruscan legend tells how one day, near the Marta River, a wise child rose up out of a ploughed furrow in the earth. Etruria's priest-kings

Figure from Chiusi

ran to the spot and the child dictated to them a sacred doctrine that they wrote down. When he finished, the child died and fell back into the earth. He was said to be Tages, grandson of the chief god Tin (Zeus), and on the field where he died, the Etruscans built their first city, Tarquinii.

Twelve city-states were: Arretium, Caere, Clusium, Curtun, Perusia, Populonia, Tarquinii, Veii, Velathrii, Vetulonia, Volsinii and Vulci.

Tyrrhenian Sea is named after the *Tyrrhenoi*, the Greek word for Etruscans.

Veii, one of the TWELVE CITY-STATES, stood 18 km north-west of Rome, to which it fell about 396 BC after a 10-year siege.

Voltumna was the chief deity of Etruria, but the exact location of his shrine is not known. Each year, the city-states' representatives met there, and the senior among them drove a nail into a temple wall. Etruscans believed that when the wall was covered with nails, the time-span of Etruria would be finished. When the Romans invaded the country, they carried off 2,000

bronze statues from Voltumna's shrine and melted them down to make coins to pay for the conquest of Etruria's ally, Carthage.

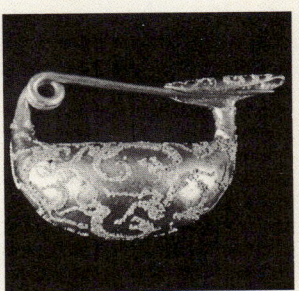

Gold pin

The beautiful bronzework of the Celts has been found in every corner of Europe – a testimonial to the extent of destruction wrought by this warrior race. Their priests, the Druids, performed mysterious rites at temples such as Stonehenge.

The Celts

It was in the 500s BC that Mediterranean traders first came into contact with the barbarous Celts, an Indo-Aryan people then centred in Switzerland and present-day south-western Germany.

The Celts later spread from central Europe, some to plunder European trade routes, others to establish a settled civilization in present-day France, Belgium, Britain and Ireland.

Warriors, farmers and metalsmiths

Below the kings, Celtic society had an upper class of warriors, the highest rank of which were priests, called DRUIDS, and a lower class of free farmers. Large family groups of Celts lived together in stockaded farmsteads, usually within reach of a fortified hill to which the whole community could flee if attacked. Women wore long, single-piece gowns, and their status varied between settlements. Men usually wore tunics or shirts, and both sexes wore cloaks as overgarments. Trousers were introduced into western Europe by the Celts.

The Celts, who had learned metal working from nomadic tribes further east, became outstanding craftsmen and Celtic bronzework of superb quality dating from the 600s BC has been found at Strettweg in Austria. Later, Celtic chiefs from central Europe traded the masterpieces of their bronzesmiths for Greek wine-drinking vessels of bronze and pottery. HALLSTATT, in Austria, became the centre of Celtic ironworking, and from there the craft spread westwards. Celtic ART also spread from its centre in Switzerland.

Gods and Druids

Among the many deities of Celtic Ireland was the Dagda, father of all, and lord of life and death. The Dagda was an ugly, pot-bellied figure mounted on wheels, who carried a monstrous club. With one end of the club he could kill nine men; with the other end he could restore them to life. Another god, Lug, a multi-skilled craftsman, was worshipped throughout the Celtic world and Welsh deities included the Children of Don, one of whom, Govannan, was a smith and brewer.

The Druids performed secret, religious and magical rites in which noon, midnight, the full moon, the oak and its parasite the MISTLETOE, played sacred roles.

Migrants and raiders

About 400 BC, Germanic tribes began squeezing the Celts out of Germany and many of them were absorbed into the various tribes then in movement across Europe. Some, mounted on horseback and armed with iron weapons, set off to find new territory in present-day Italy, Spain and France, and crossed into Britain and Ireland.

In 390 BC, the Celts invaded Etruria, sacked Rome, and plundered southwards as far as Sicily. The Romans called them Gauls, and to northern Etruria, where some of the Celts settled, they gave the name CISALPINE GAUL (Gaul this side of the Alps). The Celts continued their ravages and

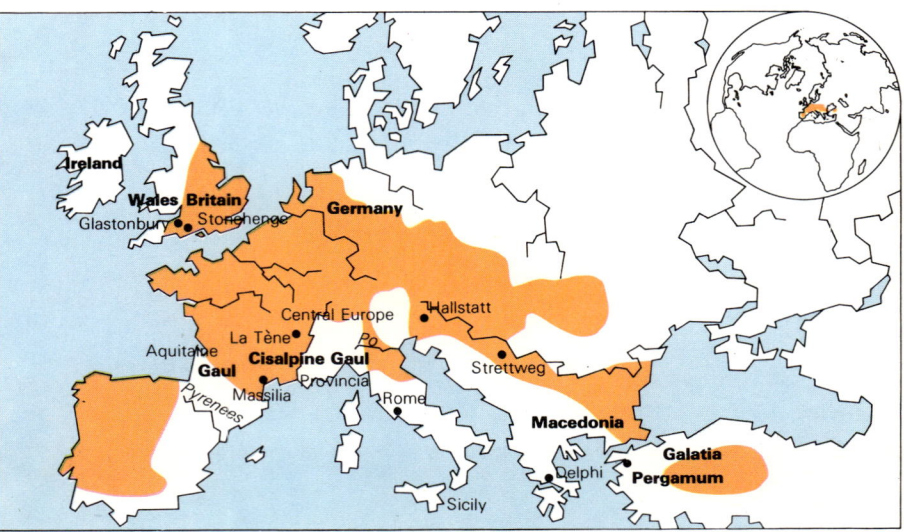

Above: This map shows the extent of Celtic migrations in about 500 BC. They later founded settlements in what are now Wales, Ireland and Cornwall.

Reference

A **Aquitani,** one of the peoples of Gaul, inhabited Aquitaine – a province created by Julius Caesar and later disputed over by England and France.
Art of La Tène, a Celtic settlement on Lake Neuchatel, Switzerland, stemmed from Greek, Etruscan and Scythian motifs. The Celts combined and modified them into highly abstract designs on metal, pottery and wood. The Celts took the La Tène culture into the lands where they settled and it is found especially in a Celtic lake dwelling at Glastonbury, England.

B **Beaker people** were Bronze Age invaders who conquered Britain's New Stone Age farmers in 2000–1600 BC. Their name comes from their custom of making decorated pots shaped like beakers.
Belgae, the northern tribe of Gaul, gave its name to Belgium in AD 1830, when it gained independence from the Netherlands.

C **Cisalpine Gaul** (Gaul this side of the Alps) was the Roman name for the Celtic province of northern Italy. It was divided into Cispadane Gaul (on this side of the Po River) and Transpadane Gaul.

Sacrifice on silver cauldron

D **Deities** of the Celts were often superhuman heroes, many being chieftain gods, some with silver hands to replace their own hands lost in battle. Celtic deities, like Celtic people, lived in a world dominated by war, craftsmanship and agriculture. Later Greek and Roman gods were integrated into the Celtic pantheon.
Druids were judges, teachers, priests and keepers of the unwritten folk lore of the Celts. They taught that at death the soul passed to another body, which lessened the fear of their warriors in battle.

G **Galatians** were Gauls or Celts who migrated to Asia Minor and settled around present-day Ankara. Their territory, Galatia, comprised parts of Phrygia and Cappadocia.

H **Hallstatt,** now a small village in Austria, is the site of prehistoric remains found in the AD 1800s. They

Below: Celts lived in large family groups in farmsteads which they defended with stockades. These farmsteads stood within reach of hill forts to which all the families in an area would flee if attacked.

in 335 BC they faced Alexander the Great in Macedonia. About 279 BC they had moved as far as Delphi, where they desecrated the sacred oracle. They then crossed into Asia Minor where they became known as the GALATIANS and were finally quelled by King Attalus of PERGAMUM.

Rome strikes back

By 192 BC the Roman army had grown in strength and marched through the old Etruscan territories to conquer Cisalpine Gaul. Then they crossed the Alps into TRANSALPINE GAUL, which extended from the Pyrenees beyond modern Belgium and was inhabited by three peoples: AQUITANI, BELGAE and Celtae (Celts) – all of whom the Romans called Gauls. During the 100s BC, the Romans took the Mediterranean coastal strip of Gaul, which they named PROVINCIA, and Julius Caesar (100–44 BC) annexed the rest of Gaul in 58–49 BC.

Before this (about 75 BC) the Belgae had invaded Britain, where earlier Celtic migrants had established Iron Age settlements. Aware of cross-channel aid between the Belgae, Julius Caesar landed briefly in Britain in 55 BC, returning again a year later.

Left: The Celts practised mixed farming, especially cereal growing and cattle raising. Although men normally wore belted tunics, Celtic horse-riders introduced trousers into Europe about 300 BC.

showed that an ironworking centre was flourishing in this Celtic territory in the 300s BC.
Human sacrifice was once practically universal, and was especially practised by the Celts in times of trouble. Julius Caesar reported sacrifices by burning, but other writers report seeing bloodstained altars. Human heads were also offered to the gods.

M Mistletoe, a parasite of many trees, was especially sacred to the Celts in association with the oak tree. Druids distributed pieces of mistletoe as charms. The Christian custom of kissing under the mistletoe at Christmas is a variation of this pre-Christian custom.

P Pergamum became a brilliant centre of Greek civilization under the Attalid dynasty about 300 BC. It was anti-Macedonian and pro-Roman, and the last king of Pergamum, Attalus III, bequeathed his kingdom to Rome in 133 BC.
Provincia (or 'the province'), the Mediterranean coastal strip of Gaul, was given this name by the Romans. It later became the French province of Provence.

Hallstattersee

S Stonehenge, on Salisbury Plain, England, is one of several major monuments in the area. The main section of the monument comprises 30 vertical rough-hewn stones standing in a circle. Lying across the top of these are 30 horizontal, touching stones. Unknown builders began constructing Stonehenge about 2600 BC.

T Transalpine Gaul became known to the Greco-Roman world about 600 BC, when the Greeks settled at Massilia (Marseilles). Rome defended Massilia against attacks by Gauls in the 100s BC.

The short life of the boy-king Alexander the Great is a dramatic adventure. At its height his empire was the largest known to the ancient world, covering over 5,000,000 square kilometres.

The Macedonians

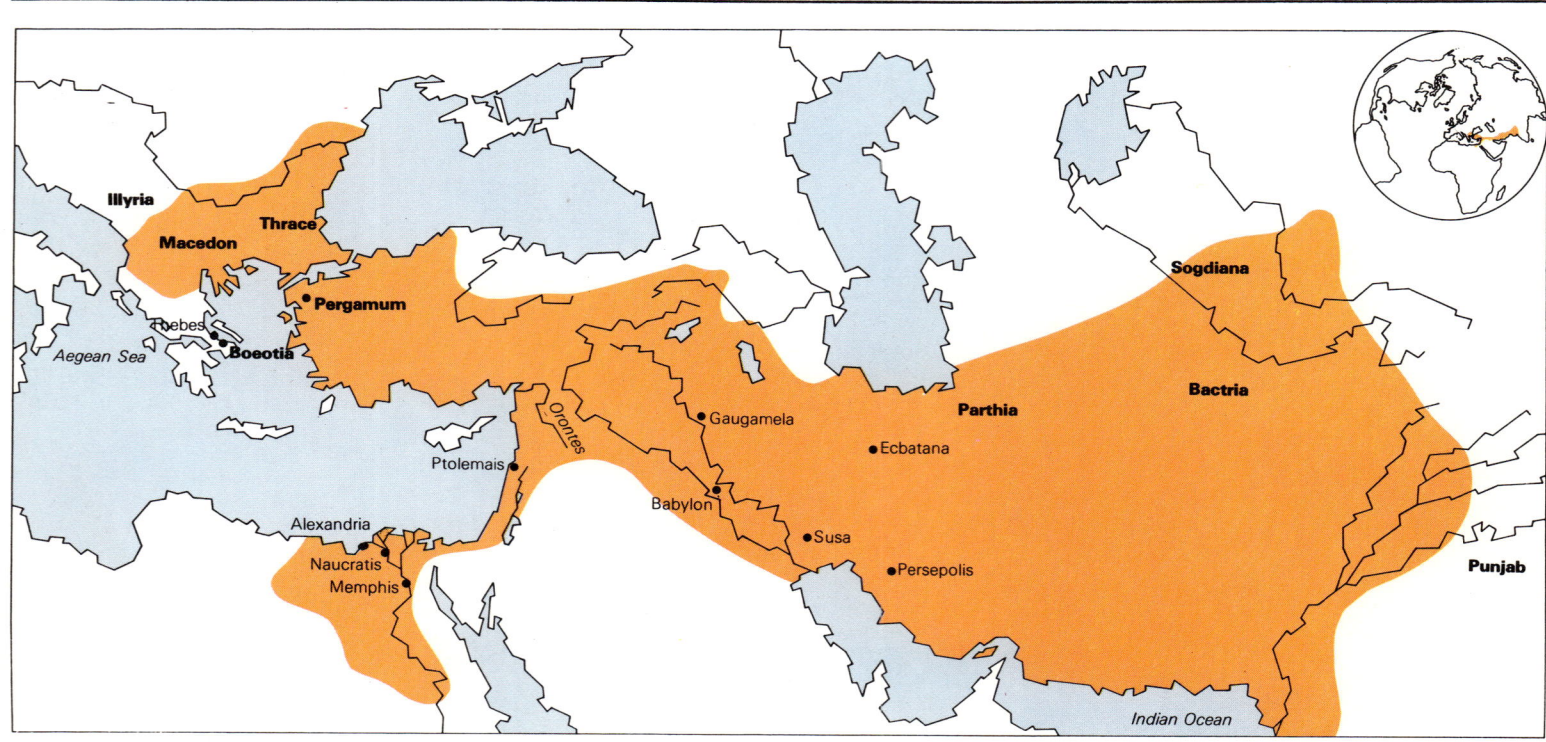

Bordering the north-western corner of the Aegean Sea was the mountainous, semi-Greek kingdom of MACEDON. The orator, Demosthenes, who died in 322 BC, represented the general Greek view of the Macedonians when he described them as useless barbarians – unable to shine even as slaves. He jibed that feuding nobles kept Macedon weak. But all this changed when PHILIP II became king of Macedon in 359 BC.

Philip II

Philip was a great general, and an accomplished politician who roused Macedonian nationalism by pursuing an aggressive foreign policy. Sure of their superiority, the Greeks did not take Philip's challenge seriously and this gave him time to hammer his recruits into a disciplined INFANTRY.

Above: The Macedonian empire begun by King Philip II of Macedon was expanded by his son Alexander into the biggest empire that the world had ever seen. The Macedonians absorbed the Persian empire and extended it into Libya, the Balkans, central Asia and India.

Right: Alexander, a fervent internationalist, forced his officers to marry foreign wives. This onyx cameo shows the heads of Alexander and Roxane, his Persian princess-wife. Rivals murdered Roxane and her son after Alexander's death.

Reference

A **Alexander's ideals** included the evolution of a multi-racial Greco-Persian empire. In order to achieve this, he persuaded or forced his generals and thousands of his troops to marry women in the Persian empire. In 327 BC he himself married Roxane, daughter of a Bactrian baron. She and her son, born after Alexander's death, were both murdered in the struggle for power that followed, although Roxane managed first to kill another of Alexander's wives, the daughter of DARIUS III.
Alexandria, apart from being a centre of learning, contained one of the '7 wonders of the world'. This was the *Pharos,* or lighthouse, built by Ptolemy II about 280 BC.
Athens came under Macedonian control in 322 BC, and thereafter diminished in importance.

C **Chaeronea,** in Boeotia, was the site of a battle in 338 BC, between the allied Athenians and Thebans, against the Macedonians, who won.
Court intrigues surrounded the assassination of PHILIP II. The king was killed by Pausanias, a bodyguard, in revenge for being ill-treated by the friends of Philip's new wife. Philip had 7 wives simultaneously, and the senior, Olympias (mother of Alexander), was wrongly accused of murdering the king out of jealousy. Several relatives and courtiers made the most of the confused period before Alexander was confirmed as king. The assassin was probably executed according to Greek custom: 5 iron clamps secured the neck and limbs of the murderer to a wooden board, while he starved to death in public.

D **Darius III** fled to Bactria when he lost the vital battle of GAUGAMELA to Alexander the Great. There the satrap murdered him and later a Macedonian officer found his body in an abandoned waggon. Alexander wrapped his own cloak around Darius's corpse and had it taken to PERSEPOLIS for royal burial.

F **Fever** that killed Alexander may have been malaria, although some ac-

Incense burner

The Macedonians

Above: In the Macedonian phalanx, soldiers kept the enemy at bay by using their very long thrusting spears. This allowed the cavalry to charge at a weak spot in the enemy line, so breaking his ranks.

Left: The Macedonian soldier, disciplined in the new tactics of Philip of Macedon, proved superior to the soldiers of Greek states to the south. Under Alexander, the Macedonian army humbled the mighty Persian army.

Below: This mosaic from Pompeii shows Darius and his Persian army in full battle. Alexander routed the Persians at Issus and Darius fled.

In 342 BC, Philip conquered THRACE, so ATHENS and THEBES hastily formed an alliance to protect themselves. But Philip routed their armies at the battle of CHAERONEA in 338 BC. Instead of punishing the defeated Greeks, Philip forced them into an alliance called the League of Corinth, which he controlled. Then, with League support, he prepared the invasion of Persia in 336 BC, but before this took place Philip was murdered by one of his own bodyguards. Despite COURT INTRIGUES, the succession passed to Philip's power-hungry son, Alexander, who speedily put down risings in Thrace, ILLYRIA and Thebes.

Alexander the Great

Alexander the Great (356–323 BC) was soon to develop the greatest empire known to the ancient world. His campaigns began when in 334 BC, he crossed the Hellespont (on the Bosphorus) with 32,000 infantry and 5,000 cavalry troops. The Persian force was quickly defeated and Alexander then marched across Asia Minor. Although the Persian king, (DARIUS III) took Alexander by surprise, he was decisively beaten and Persia began to collapse quicker than Alexander could advance. Having taken Syria and Phoenicia, Alexander entered Egypt to be acclaimed as a god. In 331 BC, he defeated Darius at GAUGAMELA, then pressed on to take the Persian capitals of Babylon, Susa, PERSEPOLIS and Ecbatana.

Alexander then turned explorer. He enticed his armies on to remote Parthia, Bactria, SOGDIANA and the Punjab. Possibly he would have gone on to China, but his weary troops forced him to follow the Indus River south to Pattala, near the Indian Ocean. There, his army divided. Part of it put to sea and sailed up the Persian Gulf, while the main body, led by its king, made the dreary march back to Persia. The two forces linked near Susa and marched on to

counts given after his death suggest that he died of drunkenness. Other scholars think Alexander may have been poisoned by those intent on succeeding to his power. According to usual custom, the army was purified from the pollution of the king's death by marching between the 2 halves of a dog that had been disembowelled. It was generally believed that at death Alexander had ascended to heaven.

G **Gaugamela** was the scene of the final battle that defeated Darius III in 331 BC. Alexander had 40,000 infantry and 7,000 cavalry while the Persian army was said to number as many as a million.

Alexander on a lion hunt

H **Herophilus,** a physician known as the 'father of scientific anatomy', studied the brain structure, distinguished between motor and sensory nerves, and took the pulse with a water clock.

I **Illyria,** a western coast state of the Balkans, was located northwards from present-day central Albania. Illyrians were mixed with Celts. They were a warlike people, prone to piracy, and no one fully conquered them before the Romans.

Infantry of Macedon were organized into *phalanxes*, a concept invented in Sparta, developed in Thebes, and perfected in Macedon. Soldiers were formed in rows to make a solid block, their task being to hold the enemy infantry by thrusting with long spears. This done, the Macedonian cavalry would charge at some spot in the enemy line, so breaking their ranks. Usually, these tactics routed Macedon's foes.

L **Legend of Alexander.** After his death, Alexander's body was set in spices in a gold coffin and placed on an ornamented chariot like the one the god Mithras was said to use. It was believed that the body would confer status on its possessor and so it was

Babylon, where in 323 BC, worn out perhaps by his effort, Alexander died of FEVER at the age of 33. The MACEDONIAN EMPIRE, the largest then known, was left leaderless.

Alexander's death brought an immediate struggle for power between his generals and relatives and half a century of foreign and civil wars followed. One general, Ptolemy, resorted to stealing the general's corpse with the hope that the LEGEND OF ALEXANDER would help to make him master of Egypt. However, most of the Indian conquests were lost to Chandragupta I and the Mauryas and Macedon and Greece slipped into anarchy, while Babylonia fell to Seleucus I. The rise and fall of Macedon had been so swift that it had almost no culture to spread abroad, although the Macedonian generals did carry aspects of Greek civilization into the lands they conquered.

Ptolemaic Egypt

It took Ptolemy 18 years to secure his position in Egypt and make himself pharaoh, although he reigned 304–282 BC and his dynasty was to last 274 years. Ptolemy founded only one new city, Ptolemais, so avoided the danger of independent city-states emerging. Everything in Egypt was methodically governed and taxed by an army of Greco-Macedonian officials and as a result the Ptolemies became the richest of Alexander's heirs. Much of their wealth was lavished on ALEXANDRIA, their capital, and this 'island' of Greek culture became for several centuries the leading city of the West after Rome.

The Ptolemies patronized Greek science and scholarship in Alexandria where they founded a museum for the study of the 'muses' – nine goddesses of the arts. They also built up two vast libraries which together held about 500,000 different rolls of papyrus books. A university was founded with several leading SCHOLARS in attendance and HEROPHILUS, a physician, founded a medical school. But outside Alexandria, Ptolemais and Naucratis, a trading centre, Egypt continued largely as before. It had merely replaced its Egyptian, Assyrian and Persian pharaohs for Macedonian pharaohs.

The Seleucids

Seleucus (321–280 BC) was the founder of a dynasty which lasted 237 years. A less prominent general than Ptolemy, he nevertheless gained the biggest share of Alexander's empire and more than any attempted to recreate the empire according to ALEXANDER'S IDEALS. Winning Babylon by 312 BC, he fought perpetual wars to extend his territory to the borders of Macedon and India.

Seleucus continued the Persian system of government. He also founded several colonies which included Antioch on the Orontes River, his capital, which became second only to Alexandria. Seleucus was assassinated in 280 BC, just as he was about to seize the vacant throne of Macedon.

Pergamum

Pergamum, a Greek city-state, managed to break away from Seleucid control and at a time of Seleucid weakness, it seized western and central Asia Minor. Pergamum's empire reached its height about the 190s BC, and Pergamum itself became a brilliant centre of Greek civilization.

Pergamum avoided being attacked by the Macedonians and the Seleucids through its friendship with Rome and when King Attalus III died in 133 BC, he bequeathed Pergamum to the Romans. By then, Macedon had already fallen to them (168 BC). The Seleucid kingdom fell in 84 BC; Ptolemaic Egypt in 30 BC.

Right: A Ptolemaic queen wearing the headdress of the vulture goddess Mut. This was the royal insignia of all Egyptian queens down to Cleopatra VII, the Cleopatra who committed suicide in 30 BC.

Below: This statue found in Thebes is of Alexander the Great.

---

kidnapped by Ptolemy, taken to Egypt and buried at Memphis. Ptolemy's son later took it to ALEXANDRIA. There, the Roman emperor Augustus saw it 300 years later.

M **Macedon** had a population of perhaps 500,000 people. Although Greek-speaking, the population was Greco-Illyrian-Thracian. It never recovered from the loss of men who went abroad with the army and did not return.
Macedonian empire. Up to Alexander's time this was the largest empire. It covered over 5 million sq km – 200 times the area of all the Greek city-states.

P **Parchment,** the prepared skins of animals (especially of calf, goat and sheep) began to replace papyrus as a writing material in the 100s BC. The name parchment is a misuse of 'Pergamum', where parchment was in early use.
Persepolis, one of the Persian capitals, was set afire by Alexander supposedly as an act of revenge for the earlier Persian burning of Athens. It is also said the soldiers wanted revenge because they had found some mutilated corpses of Macedonian soldiers.
Philip II, once hostage in Thebes, later introduced into the Macedonian army the phalanxes he saw there. Philip's remains were found in Macedon in AD 1977.

S **Scholars** at Alexandria included Aristarchus of Samothrace (collator of Homer's writings); Euclid the geometrician; and (about AD 127–141) Ptolemy, the mathematician, astronomer and geographer.
Sogdiana, on the fringes of Persia's empire in central Asia, was the location of the later cities of Bukhara and Samarkand. It formed a buffer state between Persia and the Mongols.

Thracian leg armour

T **Thebes,** the chief city of Boeotia, consistently opposed Athens. It finally joined with Athens in defence against Macedon, but Philip II conquered it.
Thrace, a land of petty kingdoms, had no Greek culture, but was famed for its music and poetry. PHILIP II seized the partly-Persian state in order to bring his armies to the Persian border. Greek states imported silver, gold, and mercenaries from Thrace.

The glory that was Rome – this city was the jewel of Roman culture. Much still remains of the Romans' work in Italy and the rest of Europe for they were skilled engineers and builders. However, for 1,000 years they were nearly always at war.

The Romans

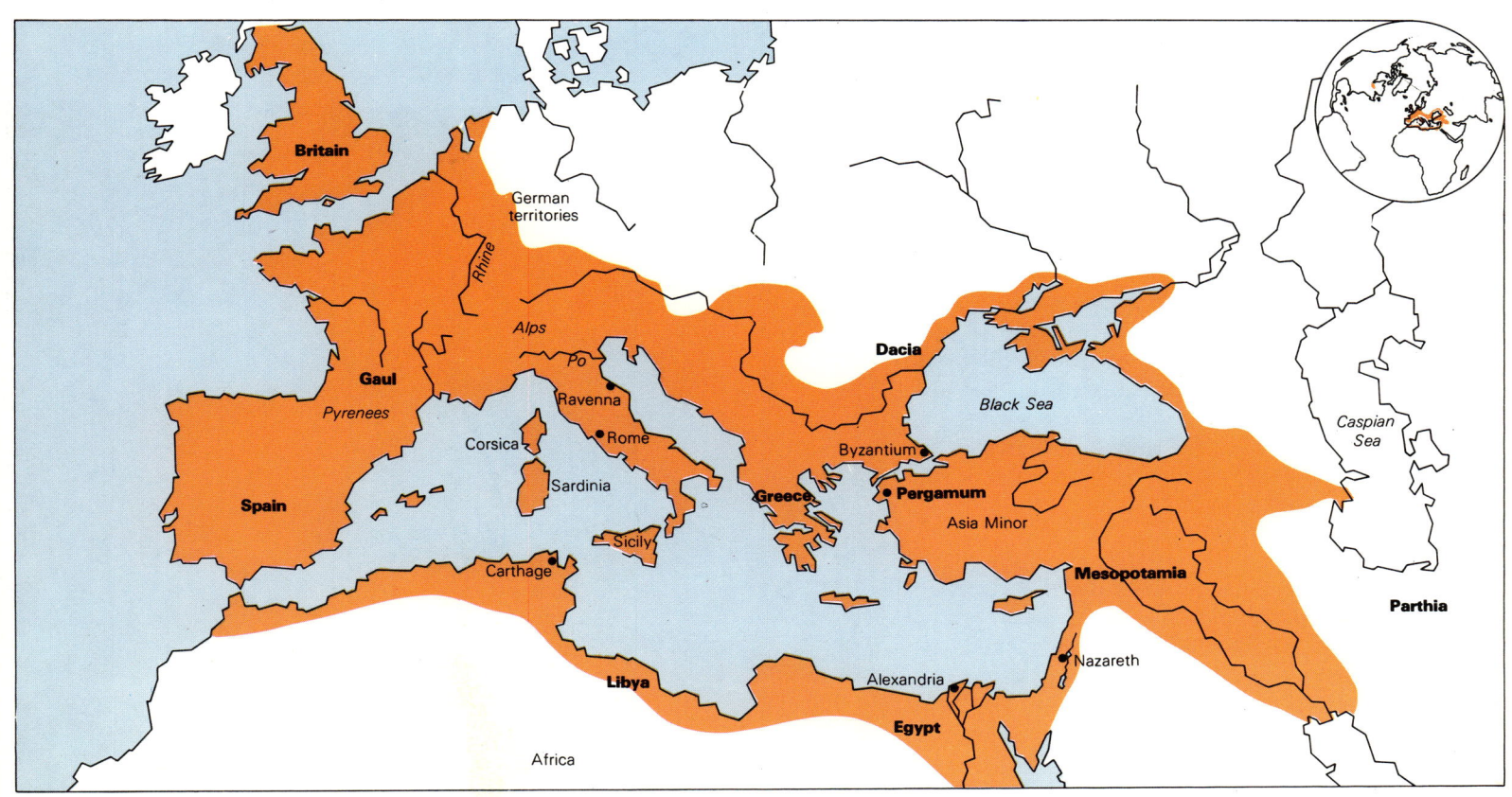

The Romans established their independence from Etruria in 509 BC, but it took them 300 years to conquer Italy. Then they spent another 300 years building up the empire to its greatest extent. Under Emperor TRAJAN it covered about 6,500,000 square kilometres in three continents and contained perhaps 60 million people. From this peak it declined for nearly 400 years. These 1,000 years of Rome were spent in almost perpetual warfare. After the city of Rome fell to BARBARIANS, the empire had another 1,000 years of life in the east. This later Roman empire, founded upon Byzantium (modern Istanbul) ended little more than 500 years ago in 1453.

Above: The Roman empire reached its greatest extent under Trajan in AD 117.

Above: In legend, a she-wolf suckled Remus and his brother Romulus, supposed founder of Rome in 753 BC. But the bronze shown was cast by Etruscans who in fact founded the city about 600 BC.

WESTERN ROME was a republic for the first half of its life and an empire for the second half. Julius CAESAR and his successor, Augustus, marked the transition at a time when the new religion of Christianity was emerging. From then the affairs of empire and church were to become closely inter-dependent.

While Roman culture borrowed heavily from Greek, the Romans were a much more practical people, excelling in government and engineering. The Macedonians took Greek civilization eastwards, but the Romans spread it in modified form throughout western Europe and the Mediterranean.

Reference

A Angles, Saxons and Jutes began to invade southern Britain in the AD 400s. This was the result of an invitation in 449 from Vortigern, a Celtic chief, to 2 Anglo-Saxon chieftains, Hengest and Horsa, to help him fight the Picts of northern Britain. The Anglo-Saxons and the Jutes were Germanic peoples who came from the present Danish-German border area and the mouth of the Rhine.

Animals kept for their products or for transport included cattle, goats, donkeys, horses, mules, pigs, poultry and sheep. Camels bred in Syria and northern Africa were often used as pack animals.

Arians were a Christian sect who followed the heresy taught by the Libyan, Arius (AD c. 256–336). He was a parish priest in Alexandria, who said that God created his Son, who was the first living creature, but that the Son was neither equal to the Father, nor eternal, but a demi-god.

Attila's Huns forced payment of tribute from the Roman emperors until AD 450, when payment was refused by Eastern Emperor Marcian and Western Emperor Valentinian III. Attila (c. 406–453) lost his campaign in Gaul in 451 and invaded Italy (452), but plague and shortage of supplies drove him back. He was called 'the Scourge of God' yet kept Roman scholars at his court and was less destructive than most BARBARIANS.

B Barbarians were to the Romans any peoples not having Roman citizenship. However, like the Chinese, the Romans constantly admitted 'barbarians' into the empire. This was either

Cast of dog, Pompeii

when they became acceptable culturally, or when they became too strong to defeat.

Barley provided fodder for farm animals, and in Egypt it was used to make beer. In the Mediterranean countries, wine, not beer, was drunk by all classes.

Burgundians moved from the Germanic territories into eastern Gaul and established a kingdom there about AD 480.

C Caesar, Gaius Julius (100–44 BC) was a Roman general and statesman. Elected praetor in 62 BC

The Romans

In the early days of the republic, citizens were divided into upper-class patricians and lower-class plebeians. For 200 years, TRIBUNES (spokesmen of the plebeians) demanded an equal share in government and in 287 BC, the plebeians at last won the right to become senators and CONSULS. But in practice this was barely possible because, as politicians were unpaid, no plebeians could afford to take on the job and senators and consuls continued to be mostly rich landowners.

The power struggle in republican Rome

Perpetual wars made the rich richer and the poor poorer. Landowners ceased to hire freemen when they could use prisoners-of-war for nothing and poverty-stricken, out-of-work peasants either crowded into the city of Rome looking for jobs, or emigrated.

When, in 133 BC the popular tribune Tiberius GRACCHUS demanded that land should be seized and given to the landless poor, he was murdered. Rome then began 100 years of riots, rebellions and civil wars, during which time the strongest men ruled. MARIUS and SULLA (see pages 10-11) were followed by other military dictators and in 54 BC, Julius Caesar seized Rome to control the whole Roman world.

The emperors

Julius Caesar was murdered because the Romans feared that he would make himself their emperor, but ironically his death in 44 BC marked the beginning of the reign of about 80 emperors. The first, Augustus, was appointed by the Senate in 29 BC. Roman politics were alive with intrigue and an emperor needed either a great deal of wisdom or a great deal of cunning and an efficient network of spies to stay in power for long. Often their lives came to a violent end at the hands of their enemies, whether by poison or a dagger, and one of the most nerve-racking jobs in the court must have been that of official food-taster to the emperor.

Amongst those who ruled the Romans well was CLAUDIUS, a gentle and wise man and a strong emperor despite the fact that he stammered and was lame. At the other end of the scale were the reigns of cruelty and terror of CALIGULA and NERO, who murdered both his mother and his wife and began the persecution of the Christians.

Below: As the empire expanded the Romans built a vast network of roads to travel along safely and quickly. Where possible they took the direct line between towns, sometimes opening up dense forests as seen below. The roads were levelled, and had foundations of sand mixed with gravel or lime and were surfaced with stone slabs. They were sometimes cambered and had drainage ditches on either side.

The city of Rome

Over five centuries Rome changed from an Etruscan border town to the capital of the West, and OCTAVIAN, or Augustus as he was more commonly known, claimed that he had turned a city of brick into one of marble. No doubt though he was thinking of the luxurious villas and ornamental gardens of the wealthy rather than the squalid slums which sheltered the poor.

Rome's unemployment situation was desperate, and those who could not get work often mobbed together to protest. The most likely area

he rose to absolute power in Rome. Although he denied any ambition for kingship he accepted the dictatorship for life. He was finally assassinated in a bid to save the republic.
Caligula (Little Boot) was the nickname of Gaius Julius Caesar Germanicus (reigned AD 37–41) because he wore a pair of soldier's boots as a boy. As an emperor, he was mentally unbalanced and cruel, and his guard officers eventually killed him out of fear.
Cicero (106–43BC) set a style in Latin prose that is still regarded as a model for the language. He was an orator and a statesman who tried to save the Roman republic from decline and was killed for his idealism.
Claudius (reigned AD 41–54) was forced to become emperor by the PRAETORIAN GUARD after the murder of CALIGULA. People who had mocked him for his limp and his stammer and thought him weak-minded were proved wrong, for he became one of Rome's strongest and most capable emperors.
Colosseum. Rome's oval shaped amphitheatre was the scene of its biggest gladitorial shows and the killings of Christians and others by wild beasts. It entertained an audience of up to 50,000 people. The Colosseum was designed by

Interior of Colosseum

Emperor Vespasian. Construction began in AD 72.
Consuls were chosen in pairs to rule the republic, preside over the Senate and lead the army into battle after Rome deposed its king in 509 BC. Both consuls could be replaced annually, which restricted their power. After the institution of the empire, 'consul' became an honorary title.

D Deities of Rome began as nature spirits and included Janus, an ancient god native to Italy who was the guardian of doors

The Romans

Above: At Bath in England, the Romans built a great bath fed by hot mineral springs rich in radium. Public baths became for the Romans important social centres.

Left: Cold-seated public lavatories provided by the government in Rome's port of Ostia date from 1,900 years ago.

Below: Emperor Claudius built the *Aqua Claudia,* a 12 km long aqueduct, to ensure that Rome had an adequate water supply.

of employment lay in building the new Rome as more and more temples, public baths, government buildings and private houses rose skywards. Allied with the building trade was the transporting of stone and marble into Rome, which became a major industry. The vast COLOSSEUM took over 200,000 tonnes of stone for facing alone. As Rome expanded to house a million people, it outgrew its port of Ostia, and Claudius enlarged it, building a new harbour and extensive warehouses.

Science and technology

Although the Romans shone as engineers, they had little interest in science, except perhaps MEDICINE. Much of their technology was a by-product of militarism, like their roads and bridges, which were built by the conquering Roman army, and their aqueducts, which carried water into garrison towns. Ingenious battering rams and slings were built to attack enemy cities, and solid fortifications to defend their own. Although the Romans devised such machines as water-powered mills using gears, they were not shy of cruelty and mainly used the labour of slaves. These slaves made it possible to keep up to 750,000 men in arms, and maintain a small ruling class living in luxury.

Arts and entertainment

Roman sculpture lacked the lithe movement of the Greek and Indian, and their massive architecture was impressive rather than beautiful. Their magnificent amphitheatres were used mainly for martial sports, as befitted a war-centred civilization, and not for drama, although the Romans produced some fine dramatists, amongst whom were LIVIUS, ENNIUS and Plautus. They likewise used Greek inspiration for their themes. The Romans had an even finer array of poets, including OVID, VIRGIL, LUCRETIUS and HORACE. Other outstanding writers were historians such as LIVY, SUETONIUS, TACITUS, Pliny the Elder and his nephew, and the master of Roman prose, CICERO.

In the market places, fortune tellers, jugglers, conjurors and musicians competed for the approval of the crown, but circuses were the most popular entertainment of all, and everyone from the emperor down went to watch horse and chariot racing, wrestling and games.

---

and gates and was portrayed with 2 faces looking in opposite directions. Later on, other important gods were borrowed from the Greeks. Jupiter, chief god; Juno; his wife and the queen of heaven; Mars, god of war, and Minerva, goddess of war, arts and crafts, correspond to the Greek deities Zeus, Hera, Aries and Athena.

Diocletian (reigned AD 284–305) was made emperor by the army and thus ended half a century of anarchy. Faced with the emergency of a German attack, he divided the empire with Maximian in 286, and with Constantine and Galerius in 293. These subordinate rulers took the title of Caesar.

E Egypt was ruled by the Ptolemies, the last of whom, Queen Cleopatra (69–30BC), cleverly kept her kingdom from Roman rule by her personal relationships with Julius CAESAR and his heir, Mark Antony (c. 83–30 BC), but OCTAVIAN refused her attentions and annexed Egypt in 30 BC.

Ennius (239–c.169BC), 'father of Latin poets', also wrote tragedies, comedies and satire. His epic history of Rome to 171 BC was written in the style of the Greek poet Homer.

External trade, though slight, was fully controlled by the state. The export of iron, bronze, arms and armour was forbidden for security reasons, but traders found ways of smuggling them out.

G Gladiators who were both freemen and slaves, fought with weapons to entertain the Roman crowds. The shows started to become popular in 264 BC and were put on either at public expense or for political or social reasons by the rich. The winner of the fight was well rewarded, and the

Gladiators

loser's fate, if he was not already dead, was decided by the emperor. He either gave a 'thumbs-up' sign, which meant the loser should be allowed to live or a 'thumbs-down', which meant death. In 73–71 BC Spartacus, a Roman slave and gladiator, led other slaves into revolt. But Spartacus was killed and 6,000 of his followers were crucified.

Gracchus, Tiberius (163–133 BC) demanded that public lands which had been taken by the rich should be seized and redistributed to the poor. At that time (133

The Romans

Above: The Roman army, a citizen militia, was raised when needed by recruiting men of property or money aged 17–60. Each legion had some 5,000 infantrymen and 300 cavalry. Through safe country a legion marched in a long column, headed by a vanguard of auxiliary troops (*above left*). These took the brunt of any sudden attack, sparing the crack troops.

Above: A hand-picked body of *equites* (cavalry) and heavily armoured pikemen with long shields came next, forming an escort for the legion or army commanders.

Above: Following the elite troops came the 'pioneer corps' and the surveyors. These carried tools for felling trees, clearing the route and pitching camp.

Above: The legion commander, usually a Senator, had a Senior Tribune as assistant. Third in the chain of command came the Camp Prefect. Picked infantry guarded them.

Economy and law

The Romans did not achieve any important advances in agricultural techniques, but kept the usual ANIMALS for their products and for transport and cultivated WHEAT, BARLEY, vegetables, olives, papyrus and flax.

For most things, the Roman empire was self-sufficient, forming its own 'common market' with private craftsmen supplying local needs. The most important EXTERNAL TRADE, which was government controlled, was in slaves, who came from the Germanic lands to the north and from the old Persian empire; and silk and spices were imported from China, incense from Yemen and pepper from India. Trading with other countries was a lengthy business, as land transport was slow and seafaring risky, so inland waterways were always used where possible.

The Roman emperors were continuously issuing new edicts. A great body of law existed but clever lawyers were nevertheless often able to baffle less-knowledgeable judges, because the law was never codified until after Rome had collapsed in the West, when the job was undertaken by JUSTINIAN.

The coming of Christianity

The first DEITIES OF ROME were nature spirits, especially of woods, waterways and wells, but the Romans later adopted new gods from Greece, from Egypt (Isis and Osiris), and from Persia (Mithras). Religion of all kinds was tolerated by the state, as was witchcraft, as long as it did not challenge authority.

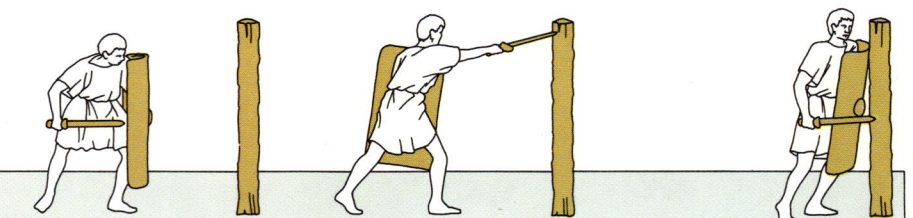

Right: A Roman recruit equipped with wooden sword and wickerwork shield practises his drill. He attacks the post as an enemy and learns to thrust.

Above: This Roman broadsword with its decorated scabbard, was found in Germany. The cross section of a curved shield (*above right*) shows that it was made of laminated strips of wood covered with sheep's felt. The shield's edge is double-stitched.

BC), the king of Pergamum died and bequeathed his country and property to the Roman people. Tiberius demanded that the property be sold to provide capital for those who should settle in the seized lands. When Tiberius was killed in a riot, his brother Gaius (153–121 BC) took up the struggle. But in 121 BC he too was killed in an election riot. Within 10 years the work of the Gracci brothers was undone.

Hannibal (247–183 BC) was a Carthaginian leader who crossed the Pyrenees and Alps to invade Italy in the Second Punic War. He reached the Po Valley with a force that included 26,000 troops, 6,000 horses, and a herd of elephants, which he planned to use like tanks. In Italy Hannibal recruited a further 10,000 troops from the Gauls. The Romans lost 3 battles to the Carthaginians, yet won eventually by invading Spain and Africa.

Horace (68–8 BC), a penniless ex-soldier, wrote philosophical poetry and prose. His works are still widely read today.

Jesus of Nazareth was probably born in 4 BC or earlier. He was a Jew and a revolutionary thinker whose followers believed him to be the Son of God (the Christ). The Jewish priestly authorities feared that Jesus' teachings and their political consequences threatened their position. In about AD 29 he was tortured and then crucified.

Justinian I (reigned AD 527–565) spent 20 years fighting the VANDALS, Huns and Franks and ruled the Eastern empire from Byzantium. He codified existing Roman law into a *Body of Civil Law*, which is still the basis of law in many western European countries.

Hannibal

Latin is one of the Indo-European languages. At first, only the people of Latium, Rome and its neighbours, spoke Latin, but later it spread throughout the Roman empire and eventually became the parent language of Italian, French, Spanish and Portuguese.

Livius (c.284–204 BC) produced translations of Greek tragedies and comedies, and a Latin version of Homer's *Odyssey*.

Livy (59 BC–AD 17) was a historian recognized as a good source on Roman times. He nevertheless in-

Above: Following the commanders came the *aquilifer* (bearer of the eagle-topped standard) wearing an animal skin. Other bearers carried standards for each *century* (company).

Above: The baggage train, comprising pack mules and ox carts, carried the army's food, equipment, tools heavy weapons, siege equipment and machinery.

Above: The main infantry column, armed with shields, pikes, broadswords and daggers, marched 6 abreast. They carried their personal equipment wedged in wooden forks.

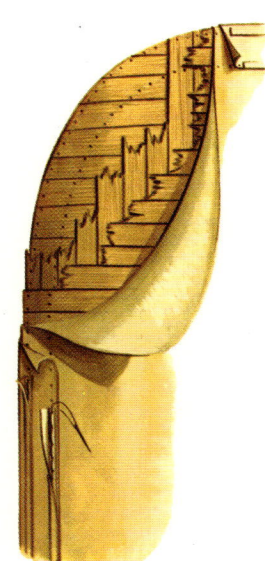

The Christians, however, had a chequered history of persecution and tolerance under the Romans. At the time of the crucifixion of JESUS OF NAZARETH in AD 30, they were insignificant in numbers, but rapidly grew as PAUL spread his teachings to Asia Minor, Greece and Italy. They first made themselves felt as a group in Rome at the time of Claudius who complained in AD 49 that their gatherings caused uproars, but they were not persecuted until Nero unjustly accused them of setting fire to Rome in AD 64.

For the next 300 years, the Christians were mostly left in peace until the reign of Diocletian (284–305), but four years after his death Galerius and Constantine I (reigned 306–337) restored their freedom of worship. As conditions improved, so the number of converts rose until Theodosius I (reigned 379–395) made Christianity the official religion in the hope of unifying his people.

The rise of the Roman empire

Legend has it that ROMULUS, the son of Mars, founded Rome in 753 BC, but in fact it was probably founded by the Etruscans about 600 BC. After its independence in 509 BC, Rome had to fight for survival against neighbouring tribes, and in 390 BC drove off an attack by the Gauls, and then another from the nearby Samnites and the Greeks of the south.

Having built up and tested its military strength and forced off its attackers, Rome then went into the attack itself. It took the granary of Sicily from Carthage in the First Punic War

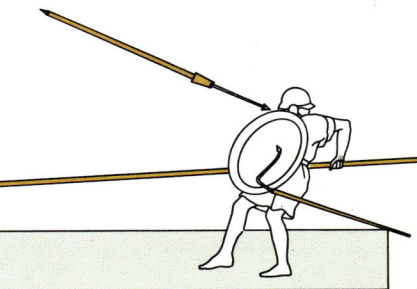

Right: A legionary goes into attack. First he throws his light javelin, then his heavier one. He then draws his sword and moves in to attack at close quarters.

---

cluded many legendary and miraculous happenings in his works.

Lucretius (94–55 BC) was a philosopher poet who had no belief in the gods, which made his works unpopular in his own times.

M Marcus Aurelius (reigned AD 161–180) was a Stoic philosopher and a soldier who won several battles in Parthia, but his armies brought the plague back to the Roman empire. He spent most of his reign defending the empire from BARBARIAN attack.

Medicine was the science that interested the Romans most, and the importance of 2 of their doctors was crucial to medical history for cen-

Marcus Aurelius

turies. Celsus (AD 14–37) wrote medical books that were not valued until long after the Roman empire had gone. Galen (AD 129–199), who was born in Pergamum and studied medicine at Alexandria, is regarded as the 'father of experimental physiology'.

N Nero was emperor from AD 54–68, but for much of that time Rome was governed by SENECA, his teacher. Nero is noted for his cruelty and he began the persecution of the Christians after a great fire which des-

troyed half of Rome. Nero held them responsible for the fire and had to rebuild Rome. Early victims of his persecution were said to have been St Peter and St PAUL, but in the end Nero's thirst for blood grew so great that his army rebelled and he was driven to suicide.

O Octavian (63 BC–AD 14) grandnephew of Julius CAESAR, took the title Augustus shortly after becoming emperor.

Odoacer (AD c.434–493), a German leader, overthrew the last Roman emperor in 476. In 493 he surrendered to another German, Theodoric the Great (c.454–526) king of the OSTROGOTHS, who executed him.

Ostrogoths settled by the Black Sea in the AD 300s, from where they were pushed westwards by the Huns. Under their king, Theodoric the Great, they became allies of Byzantium, whose emperor, Zeno, sent them to fight his rival ODOACER and recapture Italy from him in 493. Theodoric succeeded in conquering Italy, but instead of surrendering it to Zeno he kept it

The Romans

Left: Pompeii, a Greek city in Italy that came under Roman rule, was destroyed by the eruption of Mount Vesuvius in AD 79. The volcanic lava engulfed people, animals, artefacts and buildings, so preserving some of them for nearly 1,700 years until excavations began.

(264–241 BC), later adding Sardinia and Corsica to its conquests. The Carthaginian victory over Spain, heralded the beginning of the Second Punic War (218–201 BC) when the Carthaginian commander, HANNIBAL, was followed by his brother Hasdrubal across the Pyrenees and the Alps to invade Italy. But the Romans outwitted the Carthaginians by daringly counter-attacking Africa and Spain, which they conquered. In the Third Punic War (149–146 BC), Rome renewed its attack on Africa and cruelly razed Carthage to the ground.

Meanwhile, the Romans were gaining firm footholds in other parts of the world. When the Greeks appealed to Rome to free them from Macedonian rule, its troops intervened and eventually annexed all Macedonia, and 133 BC saw the addition of Pergamum to the empire, which gave the Romans a stronghold in Asia. Julius Caesar conquered Gaul; EGYPT was annexed by Octavian, who began 200 years of the PAX ROMANA, and in AD 43 Claudius annexed Britain. Interestingly enough, the Romans neglected easier conquests closer to home and it was not until 87 BC that they had most of Italy under their control.

The empire reached its height under TRAJAN in AD 117 when it occupied a vast rectangle of land networked with Roman roads with its four corners in Britain, the Caspian Sea, Egypt and Spain. Most of this territory was still held when Theodosius died in 395, but by then Rome's power was declining fast.

Division and collapse

In 395 the Roman empire was divided by agreement into West and East. The Western empire was internally weak and its borderlands were soon invaded by attackers, who were pushed further into the more prosperous Eastern empire by stronger Asian nomads. The empire fell as its strongholds and treasures were relinquished to looters. Rome was looted by the VISIGOTHS under ALARIC in 410, and finally sacked by VANDALS in 455. ATTILA'S HUNS invaded Italy in 452 but were driven back from the Po River by famine and disease. Other attackers were more successful, and included the ANGLES, SAXONS, JUTES, Franks, BURGUNDIANS and OSTROGOTHS. The onslaught culminated in 476 with the deposition of the last Western Roman emperor by the German chief ODOACER.

Above right: This artist's reconstruction of a villa in Pompeii, shows a noble's house richly decorated with frescoes, marble columns and mosaics. The ground and first floors on the left are shops rented out by the owner. In the centre is the main living room or *atrium* with a hole in the ceiling and a pool in the middle. Bedrooms lead off it. To the right of the atrium is a *tablinium* or reception room. The colonnaded area is an open courtyard containing the family shrine (*lararium*) surrounded by a covered passage or *peristyle*. Below this is (*left*) the kitchen and (*right*) the dining room (*triclinium*). Diners reclined on couches and were waited on by slaves.

---

for himself and set up an Ostrogothic kingdom centred on Ravenna. After Theodoric's death in 526, his kingdom was crushed by JUSTINIAN.
Ovid (43 BC–AD 17) is famous for his *Metamorphoses*, a collection of myths written in hexametres. He wrote mainly about love, a topic which incurred the displeasure of Augustus (OCTAVIAN), who banished him from Rome.

P Paul, earlier known as Saul, began about AD 47 to spread Christianity to Asia Minor, Greece, and eventually Rome. It is believed that he was among those beheaded about AD 67 in NERO'S persecution.
Pax Romana (Roman Peace) lasted 27 BC–AD 180, during which time Rome allowed no other powers to make war, although it fought many wars itself.
Praetorian Guard was the personal bodyguard of the emperors until it was disbanded in AD 312.

R Romulus and his brother Remus, said to be sons of the god Mars, were supposedly set adrift in baskets on the Tiber. They were then rescued and reared by a she-wolf. In the legend, Romulus later killed Remus and founded Rome in 753 BC. He then populated Rome with male fugitives and stole wives for them from the nearby Sabines. Romulus is said to have disappeared in a thunderstorm, after which he became the god Quirinus.

Nero

S Seneca (c. 4 BC–AD 65) a Stoic philosopher, playwrite and statesman, became teacher to NERO and later governed the empire for him. In AD 65 Nero ordered him to commit suicide.
Suetonius (c. AD 69–140) wrote biographies of Julius CAESAR and other emperors.

T Tacitus (c. AD 55–c.120) wrote many histories. In one of these, *Germania*, he gave the first written account of the Germanic peoples.
Trajan (AD 98–117) added Dacia and Mesopotamia to the empire. He sent so many Roman colonists into Dacia that it is still inhabited by a mainly Latin people, which explains its modern name: Romania.
Tribunes were originally officers of the Roman army

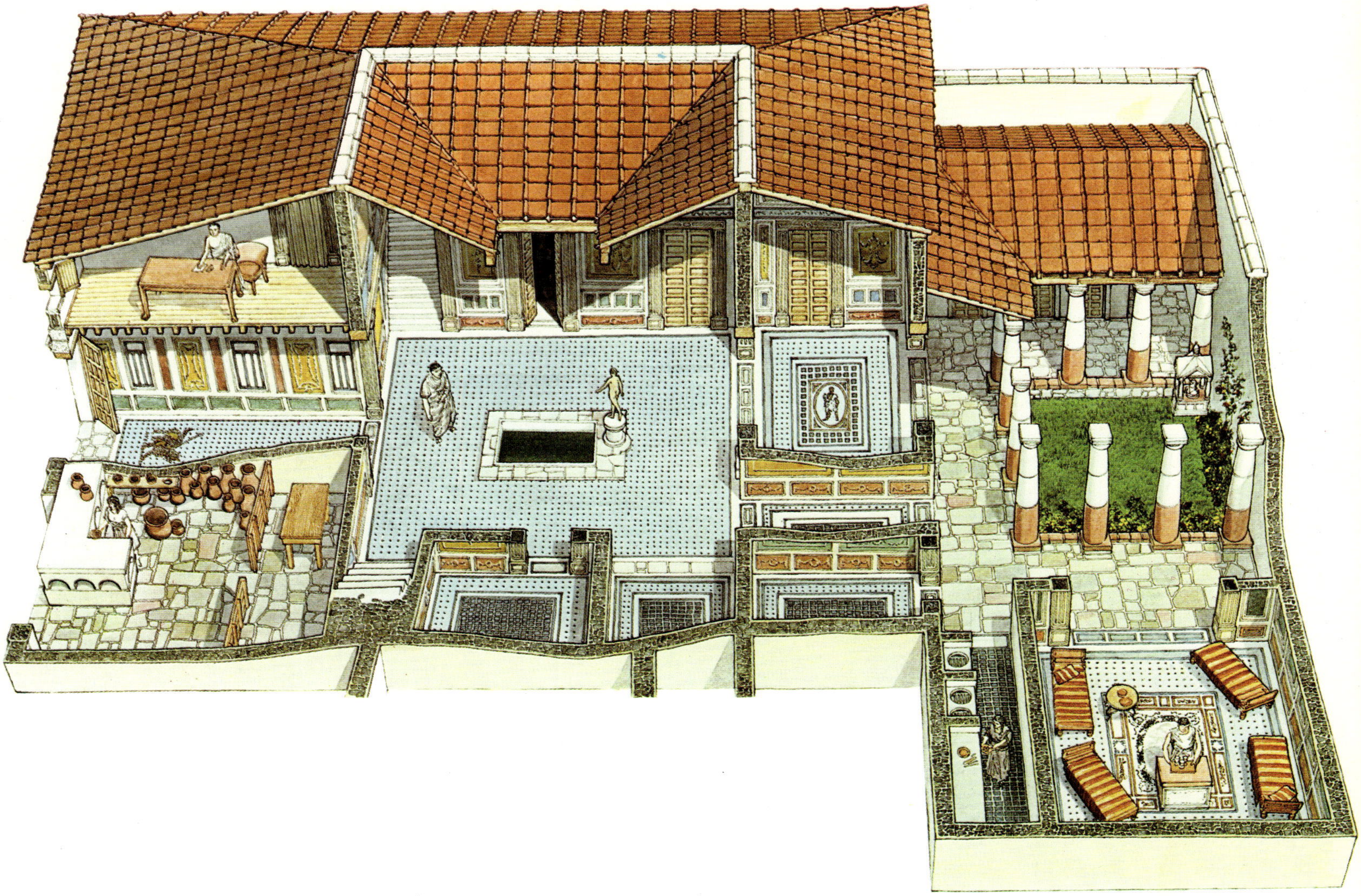

The Romans

Left: A wealthy Roman's country estate was generally self-supporting. As well as the main villa there were workshops, barns and granaries. To the right is a kitchen garden and beyond the wall are cornfields, vineyards and olive groves. The owner employed both free men and slaves as workers and a bailiff (villieus) to run the farm in his absence.

legions given the power of consuls. Later, they were men elected to an Assembly of plebeians, and by the time of Tiberius GRACCHUS they held enough power to make an emperor uncomfortable. The obvious solution was for the emperor to add the office of tribune to his other functions.

Valens was appointed emperor in the East from AD 364–378 by his brother VALENTINIAN I. He admitted the VISIGOTHS into the Eastern empire, but was later killed by them when they attacked the Eastern Roman army and destroyed 40 per cent of it.

Valentinian I (reigned AD 364–375) appointed his brother VALENS his co-emperor in the East. Although an Orthodox Christian, he allowed religious freedom to people of other religions.

Vandals were a Germanic people from present-day Denmark, Christians from the ARIAN sect that disagreed with the Orthodox Church about the nature of the Holy Trinity. They invaded Gaul, Spain and Africa, and by AD 455 their fleet controlled the Mediterranean, so they sacked Rome and took the emperor hostage. After this triumph, the Vandals warred with Byzantium, but in 533 JUSTINIAN captured their base at Carthage and they disappeared from history. Because of their sack of Rome, the word 'vandal' now means a person who mindlessly destroys.

Virgil (c. 70–19 BC) was one of Rome's greatest poets, and was greatly influenced by Homer. He wrote the *Aeneid*, Rome's national epic.

Visigoths. In AD 395 Theodosius I died and the Visigoths, who had been in his service, gave their allegiance to one of their own

Bacchus, god of wine

number, Alaric, who led them until his own death in 410. Under him the Visigoths sacked Rome in 410, but Alaric spared Roman temples and Christian churches.

Western Rome began when the Roman empire was split by agreement in AD 395 into West and East. The division ran vertically, north to south through present-day Albania and Libya. The West was by that time near its end, although the East was still flourishing.

Byzantium was the eastern capital of the Roman empire. It prospered, while Rome declined, to become the seat of the world's first Christian empire and one of the greatest centres of learning the world has ever known.

The Byzantines

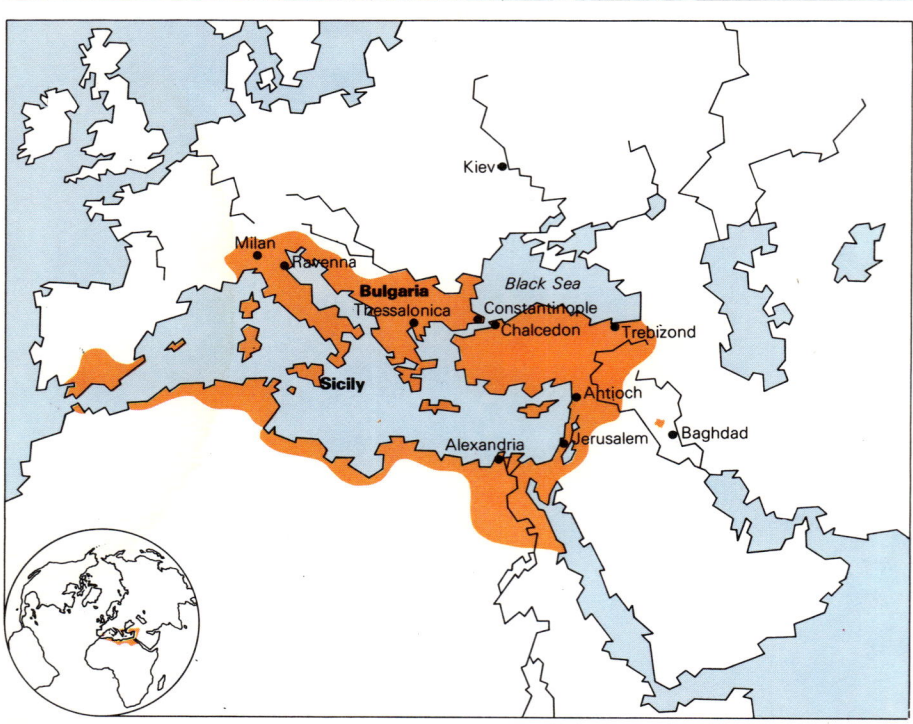

Above: Under Justinian the Byzantine empire expanded into territories belonging to imperial Rome.

Above: Justinian's head dominated the gold coins of Byzantium which became the most stable currency from Western Europe to China.

When Constantine (c.280–337) became emperor of all the Roman empire, he spent the years AD 324–30 building a new city on the site of Byzantium. This city, CONSTANTINOPLE, named after its founder, grew bigger and richer than Rome. When the empire was split into West and East in 395, it became the CAPITAL of the Eastern or Byzantine empire (often called Byzantium), and one of the world's greatest seats of learning.

Rome and Constantinople

While Constantinople flourished, Rome declined. Open to BARBARIAN attack (*see page 17*), it frequently lost even its status as the Western capital and battle-weary emperors set up temporary capitals at RAVENNA, Milan or TRIER, according to the needs of war. In religious importance, Rome's heyday had also passed because it was steeped in the cult of the old gods whose power over men's minds had gone. Christianity, the new official religion of the empire, found a safer, more sympathetic base in Constantinople, which provided the ideal capital for the world's first Christian empire.

Emperor Justinian I

Theodosius II (reigned 402–50) greatly expanded Constantinople and built a double line of defensive walls against attackers such as ATTILA, but the city reached the height of its splendour under JUSTINIAN I (*see page 20*). Justinian replaced Latin by Greek, and took to wearing a jewelled crown and silk robes in oriental style. Visitors, forced to bow or prostrate themselves before him, were overawed by the various mechanical novelties which surrounded him, including a device that hauled his golden throne ceiling-high. To promote Orthodox Christianity, Justinian punished heretics and closed the Athenian schools of philosophy.

Justinian's most lasting achievement was the codification of Roman law, which improved the status of women.

The Christian Church divides

Byzantium was obsessed with matters of religious doctrine and in 325, Constantine pronounced the Nicoene Creed, defining Christianity. But Syria and Egypt disagreed, and at the Council of Chalcedon in 451, broke away to form the separate Coptic Church. Byzantium abounded in ICONS (images) of Jesus, the Virgin Mary and various saints, but neither Church nor State approved, and in 726, Emperor Leo III (717–41) banned icons, calling them idols.

In the West, Christianity survived the empire to become the religion of its barbarian successors, and was held together by the patriarchs (or popes) in Rome. As their power grew, they

Reference

A Attila the Hun (c. 406–53) turned back from attacking Constantinople in 447, when the rumblings of an earthquake frightened his army. Some 3 tonnes of gold eventually bought him off.

B Byzantine missionaries included Cyril, inventor of the Cyrillic alphabet (861), which is still used in Russia, Yugoslavia and Bulgaria.

C Capital. DIOCLETIAN (*see page 19*) ruled the Eastern empire from Nicomedia, (near Byzantium), but in 324–30 Constantine moved the capital to Constantinople. He thought that Rome was too attached to the old religion to become the capital of a Christian empire.
Charlemagne (reigned 768–814) became sole ruler of the Franks in 771. Two years later he supported Adrian I (pope 772–95) against the Lombards, whose Italian territories he annexed, and from then on he fought perpetual wars. In 800, he hurried to Rome to prevent Pope Leo III from being deposed. There, the pope crowned him emperor.
Constantinople became rich by imposing a 10% tax on goods passing through its territory, and its gold coinage became a world currency, changing hands between Africa and China. The city held art treasures looted from many lands, and Constantine provided the rich with Roman-style houses and the poor with free bread and circuses. Constantinople boasted a Senate, hippodrome and baths, and the only cities to rival it were Thessalonica and Trebizond.

Hagia Sophia interior

E Eastern Orthodox Churches. The 3 original patriarchates, or seats of patriarchs, which were later joined by Jerusalem, were Rome, Alexandria and Antioch. The last 2 objected to Constantinople becoming a patriarchate at the Council of Chalcedon in 451, and when Constantinople was given precedence over them, Alexandria and Antioch broke away to form the Coptic Church. This later developed a 'daughter Church' in Ethiopia and in time, other independent churches, such as the Nestorian (Assyrian),

The Byzantines

Left: The construction of the magnificent Hagia Sophia (Church of the Holy Wisdom) was built by Justinian I to announce to the world that he had become head of the Church. It fell to the Muslims in 1453 and became a mosque.

resented the claim of the Byzantine emperors to be heads of the Church, and on Christmas Day 800, in a bid to make his own position more secure, Pope Leo III placed a crown on the head of CHARLEMAGNE the Frank and declared him emperor in the West.

Understandably, Pope Leo's action worsened relations between Rome and Constantinople. The final break, or Great Schism, came in 1054 when the pope of Rome and the patriarch of Constantinople excommunicated each other.

The varying fortunes of Byzantium

The Byzantine empire reached its height under Justinian, whose generals seized Italy from the OSTROGOTHS and Roman Africa from the VANDALS (*see page 87*). Besides holding Greece, Asia Minor and Egypt, Justinian dreamed of recreating the old Roman empire, but his own empire began to crumble only three years after his death, when the Lombards began a 200 year struggle to wrench Italy from the Byzantines. Eventually, both lost to Charlemagne.

The Arabs also attacked Byzantium, fired with enthusiasm by their new religion of Islam. Emperor Heraclius (reigned 610–41) used GREEK FIRE to repel their attacks on Constantinople, but Syria, Palestine, Persia and Egypt fell to them. Under the MACEDONIAN DYNASTY (867–1056), Byzantium's frontiers expanded to the Euphrates and into Bulgaria. Bulgar and Serb attacks in the north ceased when BYZANTINE MISSIONARIES converted these SLAV PEOPLES to Christianity. Russia too, was won for the Orthodox Church when a sister of Basil II (960–1025) married Prince Vladimir of KIEV in 989.

The end of the empire

In 1071, Seljuk TURKS from central Asia chased the Byzantines back across Asia Minor, and when the NORMANS took southern Italy and Sicily by 1130, Byzantium shrank to Greece and western Asia Minor. The most cruel blow came in 1204, when fellow Christians from the West interrupted their journey to fight Muslims in Palestine, and seized and looted Byzantium instead. Although the dying empire tottered on for another 250 years, it was reduced to less than 1,000 square kilometres. Church and state struggled for supremacy over an 'empire' whose population had fallen to only 60,000.

Across the narrow waters of the Golden Horn, the Ottoman Turks had replaced the Seljuks, and their leader, Sultan Mehmet II (1431–81) saw Constantinople as a 'monstrous head without a body'. In 1453, 100,000 Turks laid siege to the city for six weeks. Finally, they attacked across the Golden Horn, and the last Byzantine emperor died bravely defending Constantinople as it fell.

Below: The halo surrounding the head of Justinian proclaims his semi-divine status as Byzantine emperor. Churchmen and officials flank the emperor on this magnificent mosaic from the Byzantine city of Ravenna.

Chaldean Catholic, and Armenian.

Greek fire, a mixture of naphtha, quicklime, saltpetre and sulphur, was used in flame-throwers by the Byzantines. This 'secret weapon' was later adopted by the Arabs.

Iconoclasts (image-breakers) were active in Byzantium 726–843 with government encouragement. The anti-icon movement probably took inspiration from the Arabs.

Icons, images painted or carved as objects of worship, developed from mosaics and frescoes. Few surviving icons predate 900.

Kiev, earliest state of the eastern Slavs, flourished 900s–1200s occupying most of modern Ukraine and Byelorussia.

Macedonian dynasty began when Michael III (reigned 842–67), known as the Drunkard, was murdered by a former stable-boy of his, a Macedonian, who usurped the throne to become Basil I in 867. The dynasty's greatest warrior was Basil II (the Bulgar Slayer) who reigned 976–1025.

Normans were originally Scandinavian Vikings and land-hungry Norman warrior-nobles. They set up the kingdom of Sicily in 1130.

Ravenna became the capital of the Western empire in 402. It was also the capital of ODOACER (*see page 85*) and Theodoric (c. 454–526) and the governors of Byzantine Italy.

Slav peoples lived between the east bank of the Elbe River and Constantinople in the 500s–700s, and are believed to have originated in Polish Galicia.

Trier, capital of Belgica (Roman northern Gaul), occasionally became the capital of the Western emperors in the 290s–400s.

Turks, about AD 500, lived between Mongolia and the Black Sea. The Seljuk Turks were converted to Islam and took Baghdad in 1055, then advanced to the Mediterranean, so sparking off the Crusades. Otterman (Osmanli) Turks took over the Seljuk empire in the 1300s.

Constantine

The 'golden age' of the Tang and Sung dynasties saw an expansion of trade and the flowering of art and literature, crafts and technology. Chang-an was then the world's largest city with a population of well over 1,000,000 people.

The Later Chinese

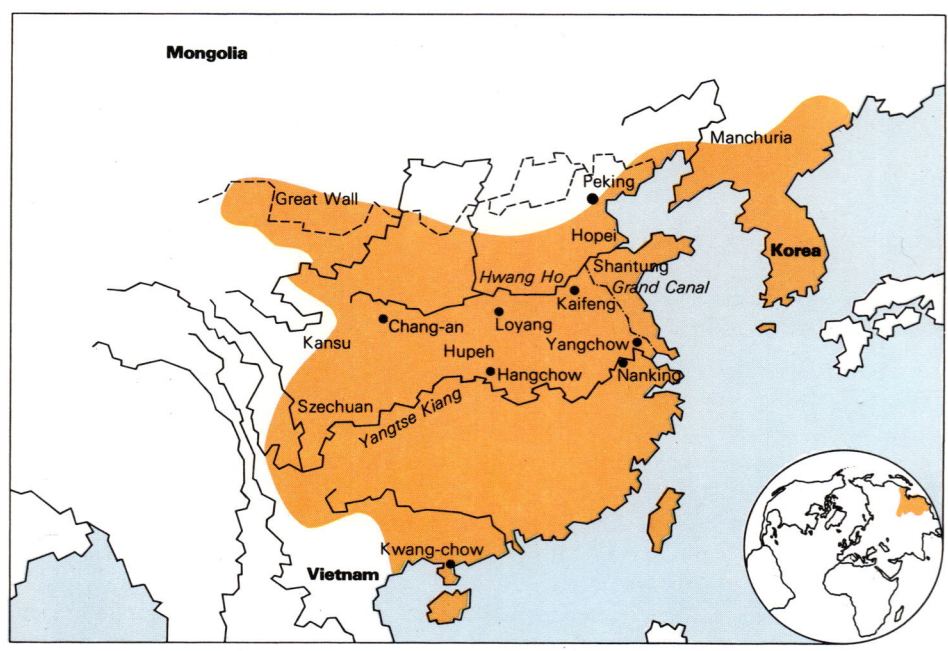

Above: Tang China, although smaller than the Han empire, had as its capital the then largest city in the world, Chang-an.

After the Han dynasty fell in AD 220, China remained disunited until the nobly-born YANG CHIEN established the Sui dynasty (581–618). He began an ambitious reconstruction drive, pressing millions of peasants into forced labour. Nearly half of the labourers conscripted to rebuild LOYANG (the eastern capital) were worked to death, and in consequence, the peasants became bitterly hostile to the regime. Yang Chien's son murdered him to inherit the throne, but lost prestige when he tried and failed to conquer Manchuria and Korea. The peasants took to arms and Sui soldiers deserted the dynasty. Then LI YUAN, a Sui army officer, seized Chang-an and became the first Tang emperor.

Tang and Sung dynasties

Tang armies conquered Manchuria, Korea, Mongolia, Tibet and Turkestan to build an empire that extended from the Caspian Sea to Korea and Vietnam. But by the mid-700s most of the border regions were lost and discontent again brought peasant revolts that weakened the dynasty. When CHU WEN, warlord of the Hwang Ho region, usurped the throne in 907, China disintegrated.

Above: This Tang figure is typical of the finer pieces of ceramic ware of the period.

The empire became reunited (with reduced territory) under the Northern Sung (960–1127), who set up their capital at KAIFENG, near the Hwang Ho in north central China. But it suffered perpetual attacks from the north, especially from the NUCHEN of Manchuria, who founded the KIN KINGDOM in 1115. When the Kin took northern China in 1127, the survivors of the Sung family fled south to establish the Southern Sung dynasty (1127–1279). Its capital, at first at Shangchiu, was later moved to HANGCHOW.

The plundering Kin massacred or enslaved the Chinese, and when the Mongols invaded China in 1211, the northern Chinese welcomed them as liberators. Southern Sung unwisely allied itself with the conquering Mongols to destroy the Kin, on condition that they would reoccupy Kin territory south of the Hwang Ho. But the Mongols cheated them out of the fruits of victory, and when Sung troops made for Loyang, their Mongol 'allies' treacherously opened the dykes of the Hwang Ho and drowned them. Then the Mongols advanced into Southern Sung China and established the Yuan (Mongol) dynasty.

Social and economic life in Tang China

With the Tang dynasty (618–907), China entered a 'golden age' and its capital, CHANG-AN, became the world's biggest city. Learning from mistakes made by their predecessors in the short-lived Sui dynasty of 581–618, the early Tang emperors tried to improve the lot of the peasants without antagonizing their powerful landlords. The peasants were demanding a redistribution of land, and to appease both factions the emperors

Reference

C Chang-an (now Sian), capital of Tang China, was then the world's biggest city with well over 1,000,000 people. Like other major Chinese cities, it attracted thousands of foreign merchants. The square-walled city was built on the grid pattern.

Cheng Ho. Several reasons have been suggested for the ending of Admiral Cheng Ho's trading missions. 1) They cost too much. 2) Shortly after the death of Timur the Lame (1406) interruptions to the central Asian trade routes ceased. 3) Having 'shown the flag' in the Indian Ocean, China's need for political prestige was satisfied. 4) Japanese piracy became a threat.

Chu Wen, most powerful warlord of the Hwang Ho region, deposed the last Tang emperor in 907. But he failed to keep China unified and until the rise of Northern Sung in 960, it was split into 5 dynasties: Later Liang, Later Tang, Later Tsin, Later Han, Later Chou.

Chu Yuan-chang (1328–98) a peasant's son orphaned by plague, became a monk and conspired with the White Lotus secret society to form the Red Turbans, a band which sought to overthrow the rich. But his wealthy enemies persuaded him to join them in an all-Chinese attack on the Mongol overlords and in several battles between 1355 and 1368 he beat the Mongol armies and took Peking without opposition. The Mongols fled back to Mongolia and in 1368 Chu Yuan-chang became the first Ming emperor.

Copper coins changed hands in 'strings' for large amounts. One tonne of copper made about 300 strings. Each string held 1,000 of the round coins with a square hole, called *cash*.

F Fire guns were long bamboo tubes filled with gunpowder.

G Gunpowder, invented in Tang China, was at first used only for firework

Sampan on Yangtse Kiang

gave them the territory that had gone to waste during the Sui civil wars. They kept rents and taxes within reasonable limits and avoided taking men for forced labour during busy periods of the farming year. Even so, they managed to cut new irrigation canals, improve the quality of livestock, grain and textiles, and wipe out crop-destroying locusts. They developed water transport to bring trade directly into the new towns that sprang up along the river banks.

Foreign trade also expanded. Nomads from the north brought furs and skins strapped on horses or camels to the border towns, and caravans from central Asia and further west carried jade, carpets and other commodities into Tang China. Arab and Persian ships sailed to the ports of southern China loaded with drugs, gems, pearls, spices, and other luxuries. The foreign ships carried away bronze mirrors, ironware, PORCELAIN, silk and tea. Trade stimulated the demand for MONEY, and each year, the Tang government put into circulation another thousand tonnes of COPPER COINS.

Town planning was a feature of Tang China. From Chang-an, good roads led to Hopei, Hupeh, Kansu, Shantung and Szechuan provinces. Loyang stood at the hub of the Grand Canal, and the great trading city of Yangchow stood at its confluence with the YANGTSE KIANG. Kwang-chow (Canton) became the leading seaport.

Right: This large blue and white bowl is characteristic of ceramic ware of the Ming dynasty. Contrasting sharply with the finer but plainer Sung ware, Ming 'blue and white' was widely copied in Japan, Persia and south-eastern Asia. Shipped to the Netherlands it inspired the Delft porcelain of Holland.

Below: The picture shows part of the Rainbow Bridge from Chan Tse-tuan's silk scroll painting *The Ching Ming Festival on the River*. It is fairly representative of the Sung dynasty style.

Technology under the Sung

The Sung dynasty (960–1279) heralded China's 'silver age'. Sung China was a weak military power compared with Tang China, but to compensate, it became the world leader in military technology, and one of its achievements was the development of the use of GUNPOWDER, which had been discovered by the Tang.

Yuan and Ming dynasties

The greatest of the Yuan emperors was KUBLAI KHAN, who moved the Chinese capital to Peking. Marco POLO, the Italian traveller, visited him there and returned to Europe with stories that made him a legendary figure in the West. Although Kublai Khan admired Chinese culture and ruled well, later Yuan emperors were less able. Agriculture declined as waterways fell into disrepair, and resistance to the Mongols increased.

The Chinese rebels were eventually united under the leadership of the Red Turbans, who defeated several Yuan armies. In 1368, despairing of holding China, the Mongol army withdrew north of the Great Wall and the Yuan dynasty crumbled away.

CHU YUAN-CHANG, a poor peasant-monk turned rebel commander, took Nanking and made himself the first Ming dynasty emperor. The Ming soon restored prosperity, but eventually, they too came up against the irrepressible power of the peasants. A 17-years' PEASANTS' WAR (1627–44) against the Ming dynasty whittled away China's internal strength, while from abroad, the Japanese raided shipping and battled with China for control of Korea.

---

displays. Sung China used it to produce bombs, rockets, flame throwers, and the power for FIRE GUNS.

H **Hangchow,** capital and hub of Southern Sung's commerce, became one of the richest and largest cities in the world. There, life was easier than in the cold, wind-swept Hwang Ho region. With the move to the south in 1127, the Sung way of life changed. Marco POLO claimed that the Southern Sung fell to the Mongols because they were too busy paying attention to women to be warriors. Hangchow offered luxury international shops, popular entertainment, fashionable restaurants, and tea houses with 'sing-song girls'.

K **Kaifeng,** the Northern Sung capital, was also called Pienching, Pien-liang, and Yeh. A colony of Jews built a synagogue there in mid-Sung times.
Kin kingdom was established by the NUCHEN in 1115.
Kublai Khan (1216–94) grandson of TEMUJIN (1162–1227) who was known as Genghiz Khan, nominally ruled the whole Mongol empire from eastern Europe to China. His actual rule was confined to China and Mongolia. Kublai did not interfere with Chinese culture, which he admired. He was followed by 7 less effective Yuan emperors.

L **Li Po** (701–762) is often considered to be China's greatest poet. His poems, frequently written when drunk, reflect the freshness of the passing moment.
Li Yuan, first Tang emperor, reigned 618–627. He was appointed by his son, who overthrew the Sui dynasty with the help of Mongol Turks.
Loyang, capital of the Eastern Chou and Eastern Han, became a subsidiary capital of Tang China.

M **Malacca,** founded by a fugitive Malay king

Chinese fresco, AD *700s*

Ante-room of tomb, Loyang

28 The Later Chinese

The economies of Yuan and Ming China
When the Mongols conquered China they made little impact on its cultural tradition apart from introducing NORTHERN DRAMA, and soon adopted Chinese ways.

The Mongols did nothing to further the Chinese economy, and when the Ming emperors succeeded them, this was their first task. Vast 'factories' were set up to mass-produce porcelain, which became China's export, and the Ming sent large trading fleets under Admiral CHENG HO off to Vietnam, India, Persia, Arabia, and eastern Africa. But these voyages stopped abruptly when foreign traders proved willing to exchange their products with the Chinese in the Malayan port of MALACCA. A constant hazard for Chinese coastal settlements and shipping came from Japanese pirates, and the Portuguese seizure of Malacca in 1511 convinced the Ming emperor that European traders were no better than the Japanese pirates.

Such was the fame of Chinese porcelain in the European markets that it became highly prized and a number of potteries tried to copy it – the Chinese fashion of decoration on pottery became very popular. For some wealthy people, landowners and noblemen in England, copies were not good enough for them. They sent orders direct to China for complete dinner services and other pieces of the marvellous porcelain. They even went to the lengths of sending engravings, such as bookplates, or miniature paintings of their family coats of arms and mottos to be placed on their custom-ordered porcelain. It took nearly two years for these heraldic orders to be completed and the porcelain delivered. When the drawings supplied to the Chinese were not sufficiently clear some curious heraldry resulted – they copied what they thought they saw, even at times down to the instructions on the drawings, which appeared on the final porcelain.

Religion and the arts
Indian Buddhism had reached China during mid-Han times, but did not become popular until the introduction in 520 of Chan (Zen), a more practical kind of Buddhism, which spread rapidly throughout the land. Buddhism did not replace Confucianism and Taoism; it coexisted with them and the Chinese combined all three religions, together with the cult of their ancient deities, into one integrated system of worship.

Above: The world's oldest printed book, the Buddhist *Diamond Sutra*, was block printed in China in AD 868. Moveable type printing, experimented with by the Chinese, was accomplished by the Koreans in the 1300s.

Right: Mongol horsemen under Kublai Khan swept down upon China during the closing years of the enfeebled Sung dynasty. Although Kublai showed little mercy in conquering China, he respected Chinese culture and governed the country well.

---

about 1403, quickly became rich from foreign trade. Chinese junks sailed there to sell their wares and return to China with Indian, Persian, Arab and European goods. Through Malacca, Islam became part of the Malay culture. The Portuguese took the port in 1511.

Manchus was the later name of the NUCHEN.

Money. As more money circulated in Tang China, reflecting increased prosperity, the weight and bulk of strings of copper cash made them difficult and risky to transport. To avoid the problem, merchants issued 'deposit certificates'. These passed instead of money. Later Tang governments issued their own certificates. The Sung took the system one stage further, issuing paper money.

Northern drama developed during Yuan times, when over 500 plays were written. Typical Yuan plays had a prologue, 4 acts, and an epilogue. Most were tragedies. Male actors portrayed set characters of both sexes.

Nuchen (also known as Jurchen, and later as Manchus), a Manchurian tribe, founded the KIN (or Chin) kingdom in 1115. They were then hunters and fishers, just settling

Women making silk: Sung

to a semi-farming way of life. Having seized northern China from the Sung, they were conquered by the Mongols. Later (as the Manchus) they seized Ming China and ruled from 1644–1911.

Peasants' war (1627–44) against the last Ming emperor was the biggest internal upheaval in Chinese history. The peasants fought under the slogan 'Equal distribution of the land among rich and poor'. The peasants toppled the dynasty, but it was the MANCHUS who profited by its collapse.

Peking (Cambaluc) was the Yuan capital (1279–1368). After a brief break it became the Ming capital in 1421, and has remained the capital of China except for brief periods during the Japanese and civil wars of the present century.

Polo, Marco (c. 1254–1324) became the most famous traveller to take the silk route to China. He travelled over much of Asia in the service of KUBLAI KHAN. His book, a marvellous mixture of fact and fancy, was written later, when a prisoner-of-war in Italy. To sell the book, he

Tang architects built Buddhist temples on a palatial scale and their literature concentrated on romantic tales and religious or supernatural themes. The dynasty produced China's two greatest poets: LI PO and TU FU. In Sung times, village groups gathered to hear priests read Buddhist tales known as Pien-wen. This began the tradition of story-telling to provide popular entertainment.

Kuan-yin (goddess of mercy) and Buddhist saints caught the imagination of Chinese Taoist – Buddhist artists, who reached their peak in the Sung dynasty with the mountain and water landscapes that still symbolize China today. Chinese porcelain also reached unsurpassed standards with SUNG CERAMIC ware and potters used coloured glazes and often took their shapes and decorative motifs from Persian metalwork and Greek designs.

The end of the Chinese dynasties

During the long period of Ming China's internal collapse, the Nuchen again threatened the northeastern border. As the MANCHUS (taking their name from Manchuria) they fought the Ming for 30 years. Finally, they took PEKING and founded the Manchu dynasty (1644–1911). The Chinese hated and despised their conquerors, and the Manchu retaliated by making them wear Manchurian clothing and tie their hair into pigtails as a badge of servitude. Chinese civilization stood still under the Manchus and China slowly degenerated into a backward area, sheltered only by the illusion of a cultural and technological superiority that had actually been lost to western Europe.

---

inserted many untruths into his story. By chance he wrote accurate accounts about aspects of Asia which were at that time unknown, but he also described unicorns, dog-headed men, wizards and giant rubies. Medieval Europeans rejected much of what was actually true, preferring to believe the fantasies.

Porcelain, mass produced in vast quantities in Ming China, went mainly for export. In one year (1643), China shipped some 130,000 pieces to the Netherlands alone, where it inspired the creation of Delft china. Ming white-glazed porcelain with blue decoration was imitated in Japan, southeastern Asia and Persia.

Chinese likeness of Marco Polo

Printing. Forms of block printing in China probably go back to the 200s BC and true printed pieces date from very early Tang times. Moveable type printing, experimented with by Pi Sheng in China, was successfully accomplished by the Koreans, who set up a type foundry in the 1300s. There was probably no feedback between East and West in this area and when Johann Gutenberg began to print with moveable type in Germany about 1440, it was most likely an independent development.

R **Red Turbans,** see CHU YUAN-CHANG.

S **Sung ceramic** ware was valued outside China for its shape and colouring. Arab rulers favoured the leaf or bluish green *celadon* ware, which they believed cracked or changed colour if poison touched it. This supposedly enabled them to escape assassins.

T **Tu Fu** (712–70) a poverty-stricken Tang poet, wrote about human suffering. His poems are longer and deeper than LI PO's, but lack their freshness.

Y **Yang Chien,** first Sui emperor, tried to keep people contented by providing public spectacles much as the Romans had done. He is said to have kept 30,000 performers and built special sites for public audiences.

Yangtse Kiang, according to Marco POLO, carried 200,000 craft upstream every year – 'more wealth and merchandise than all the rivers and seas of Christendom put together'.

The philosophical teachings of Hinduism and Buddhism created an atmosphere in which art, literature and science flourished. The Ajanta cave paintings, the *Kama Sutra*, Angkor Wat and the introduction of yoga all date from this period.

The Later Indians

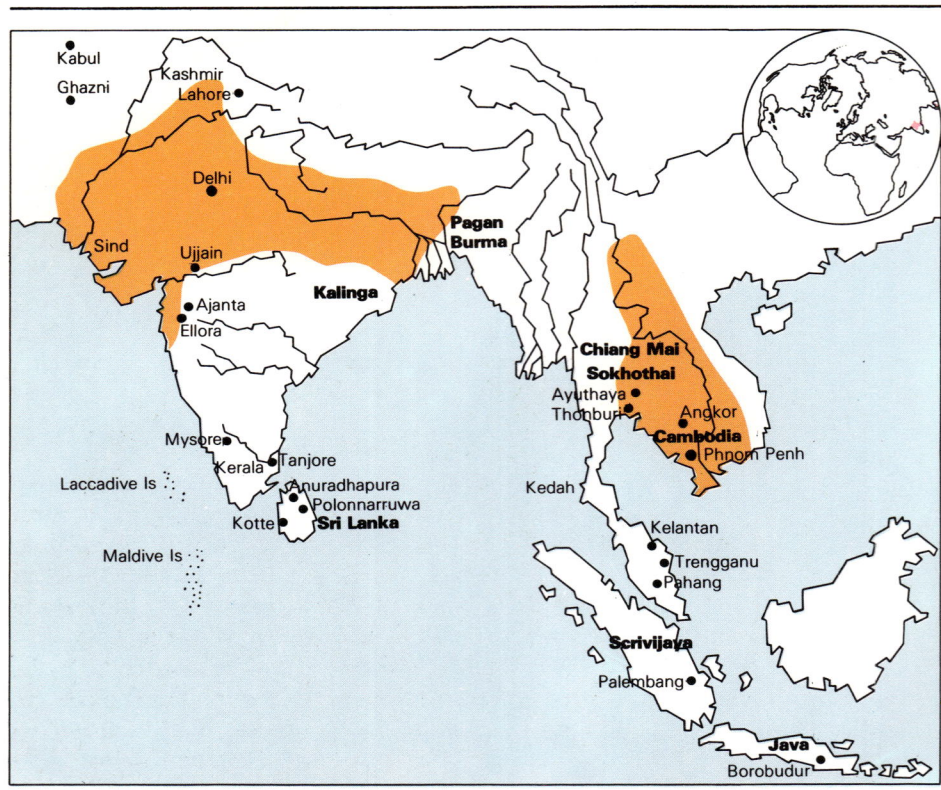

Northern India entered a new era of civilization under the Hindu GUPTA DYNASTY (AD 320–c.500). Chandragupta II (reigned 375–415) brought many small states into a confederation that extended from coast to coast. Gupta India saw the revival of Hinduism on a higher philosophical plane. With greater knowledge of anatomy, yoga developed, its disciples seeking to achieve physical, mental and spiritual harmony. Art, literature and science flourished. Indian achievements in mathematics made possible the later scientific revolution of the Europeans.

Religion and art in Gupta India
With the introduction of iron axes into Gupta India, vast areas of forest land were cleared and

Above left: The map shows the Gupta empire about 400 with its leading city of Ujjain, and the Indianized civilizations that flourished in Sri Lanka, Cambodia Malaya and Indonesia during the next 1,000 years.

Above right: A sari-clad woman weaves on a simple loom. The sari, a single length of unsewn material dyed in pleasing colours and patterns, symbolizes India's unchanging cultural pattern.

new villages sprang up. The peasants who settled there were converted by Hindu priests who brought them iron ploughs and scientific farming knowledge as well as the supposed magical power to protect the village. Buddhist monks had become too comfort-loving to serve these poverty-stricken rural areas which could not afford the costly temples and monasteries they deemed necessary.

The Gupta period produced a wealth of outstanding literature. Sudraka, an early Gupta dramatist, described in *Mricchakatika* ('Clay Toy Cart') the pleasures of middle class people in the leading Gupta city of Ujjain. He caricatured the racy underworld life of thieves, gamblers, courtesans and political rebels. In the *Kama Sutra* of

Reference

A Ajanta and Ellora. In the first 700 years AD Buddhist monks at Ajanta adapted 28 natural caves into monasteries of outstanding Buddhist art. More caves were cut by Buddhists and Hindus at nearby Ellora, including the huge Kailasa temple, with its sculpted figures, passages and chambers. The Kailasa temple was cut 30 metres downwards out of solid rock.
Angkor was the jungle site of several Cambodian capitals, the earliest dating from 802. It reached its peak under Jayavarman VII (reigned 1181-c.1219) who

Ajanta

built the vast city of Angkor Thom. The city was surrounded by 13 km of walls and moats, with 5 gated avenues leading to the Bayon, its central temple. Here the head of the god Lokeswara surmounted each gateway. Angkor's population of a million was self-sufficient in rice because of the advanced irrigation system constructed by the Khmers. In 1431 the city was sacked by the Thais, and the Khmers moved their capital to Phnom Penh.
Aryabhata, a Hindu astronomer mathematician,

was reasonably accurate in his theories concerning the earth's shape, rotation and revolution. Other Indian astronomers were able to forecast eclipses correctly.

B Borobudur, in central Java, is a vast stupa-temple built in the 800s on a natural mound. It represents in stone the Buddhist concept of the cosmological system. It has 6 square terraces in diminishing tiers, topped by 3 circular terraces. Several small bell-shaped stupas cap the huge structure.

C Cholas established a small kingdom around Tanjore (Thanjavur) in southern India about 800. Rajaraja I (985-1012) and his

Buddha statue: Borobudur

recorded about 405 by the visiting Chinese Buddhist monk, FA-HSIEN.

Scientific achievements
Indian mathematicians had clear concepts of abstract numbers. They developed algebra and trigonometry and devised the system of numbers now used by the whole world (the system of nine digits and a zero). This numeral system found its way to Alexandria in the 500s, but it took another 1,000 years for it to reach northern Europe and gain acceptance there.

The Iron Pillar of Delhi, a seven-metres length of rustless iron cast about 400, is a tribute to Indian metallurgical skill. The rustlessness of the pillar is due to the great purity of the metal, which could not have been achieved outside India until the mid-1800s.

The astronomer Aryabhata also made a great step forward for science when his studies led him to the conclusion that the earth was a rotating sphere moving around the sun.

The end of the Guptas
Gupta India fell into decline by 500, when Hunas, or WHITE HUNS invaded from central Asia. Although the Guptas eventually pushed them back into Kashmir and the north-west, their efforts heralded the end of the dying dynasty. North Indian civilization achieved a brief rebirth under HARSHA (reigned 606–647), who patronized Sanskrit literature though he favoured Buddhism. This divided loyalty cost him his life when jealous brahmins (priests and scholars) egged on his own soldiers to kill him. His death brought about the final disintegration of northern India.

One thousand years of Muslim domination
In the early 700s the Arabs took Sind, the first Indian stronghold to fall in the Muslims' gradual but persistent infiltration into India. This was typified by the determination of Mahmud of Ghazni, ruler of Persia-Afghanistan (997-1030), a fanatical Muslim known as the Idol-Breaker who raided India year after year until his death. He was followed by Qutb ud-din Aibak, a former slave from Turkistan, whose conquests led to the setting up of the SULTANATE OF DELHI (1211–1526). After this most of India passed under the rule of the MUGHALS (Mongol Mus-

Vatsyayana, love was dealt with in an innovatory way and became both an art and a science. KALIDASA reflected the typical preoccupation of the Gupta dynasty writers in his *Shakuntula* where he told a story of royalty, hermits, dense forests and the intervention of gods and demons into human affairs.

Although most of the treasures of early India have been lost, several of the Buddhist-Jain-Hindu cave temples of AJANTA AND ELLORA, which were constructed during Gupta times, contain colourful wall-paintings which have miraculously escaped decay. These portray the lively Gupta court life with dancers, musicians, actors, acrobats and magicians in attendance. The vigour and prosperity of Gupta India was

Above: A village barber shaves his customer, who inspects the result in a mirror. The barber's trade was highly esteemed in the village, where he traditionally acted as matchmaker in marriages.

---

son Rajendra (1012-44) extended the kingdom into an empire that included Kerala, Mysore and Kalinga. The Cholas attacked the SAILENDRA in SRIVIJAYA, and conquered the Laccadive and Maldive islands and parts of Burma and SRI LANKA. They built magnificent temples which are still standing at Tanjore.

F **Fa-hsien** (c.399-414) was one of several Chinese Buddhist travellers whose writings provide records of events in the Indianized world. During Chandra-gupta II's time, he travelled to India in search of authentic copies of the Buddhist scriptures. He reported that most Indians had become vegetarians and that travellers could move throughout India unhindered by bandits or bureaucrats. He also commented that northern India had a just and tolerant government.

G **Gupta dynasty** established itself in Magadha, the centre of the earlier Maurya empire by 319, but its power had ebbed away by about 500-600.

H **Harsha**, who ruled 606-647, befriended Hsuan Tsang, a Chinese Buddhist pilgrim whose writings provided much of our present knowledge about the king and his times.

K **Kalidasa**, greatest of Sanskrit dramatists, is generally supposed to have lived about 400, in the time of Chandragupta II. In addition to his greatest play, *Shankuntula*, he composed epics and poems.

M **Mughals** formed a Mongol Muslim dynasty in India. They were established by Baber (a descendant of Genghiz Khan). He became king of Ferghana in 1495, fought the Uzbeks, and in 1504 took Kabul. In 1526 he invaded India, ended the SULTANATE OF DELHI, and replaced it by the Mughal dynasty.

P **Parakrama Bahu I** (reigned c.1153), a great Sri Lankan builder of temples and palaces, also restored its ancient irrigation system. He is quoted as saying 'None of the water that comes from rain must flow into the ocean without being made useful to men.' He ruled a flourishing Buddhist civilization from Polonnaruwa, but his fore-

Gateway at Angkor Thom

32 The Later Indians

Left: A Buddha sits serenely in a niche in the vast brick-built monument of Borobudur in central Java. Built about 800 by the Sailendra dynasty, Borobudur began as a natural earth mound around which the monument was constructed. The terrace walls are carved with scenes depicting the lives of the Buddha and Buddhist saints. Borobudur represents in stone, the Mahayana idea of the universe.

lims) for 200 years, but even they did not fully conquer the south, where several independent kingdoms flourished, notably the CHOLAS.

The Cambodian empire of the Khmers

Cambodia came under the influence of the Indians about AD 100, when the kingdom of Funan was founded by Kaundinya, a brahmin known as King of the Mountain. Funan was the basis for the Buddhist-Hindu empire of the Khmers, whose capital was built at Angkor in 802 and reached a population of a million.

Below: Ritual bathing in the holy Ganges River at Benares has been practised by Hindus for perhaps 2,000 years or more. Bathing begins before dawn and is over by early morning. Hindus hope that after death their cremated remains will be finally thrown into the Ganges.

At the height of its achievement, the empire was ruled by Jayavarman VII (reigned 1181–c.1219), who was famous for his highly sculptured temples and palaces. The Bayon was his most extravagant temple dedicated to the god Lokeswara, who combined four personalities: Siva, Vishnu, Buddha, and Jayavarman himself. The god was represented 200 times on the temple.

The king's architectural excesses exhausted the Khmers and they eventually fell to the newly emerged Thai kingdom. Encouraged by KUBLAI KHAN (*see page 27*) the Thais constantly attacked Angkor, and sacked it in 1431. The Khmers retreated and abandoned their fabulous capital to the jungle.

Malaya and Indonesia

Several Indianized kingdoms grew up in Malaya and Indonesia, especially the empire of SRIVIJAYA. This spread from Palembang in southern Sumatra in the 600s to control most of Malaya by 775. Java too was Indianized by the SAILENDRA dynasty, who in the late 700s built Borobudur, a huge Buddhist stupa, or monument, in central Java. When the Sailendra lost Java, they took over Srivijaya, but their power waned by the 1000s, and their empire disintegrated. Nearer the mother country, the Indian Tamil Chola kings invaded Buddhist SRI LANKA where they introduced Hinduism.

---

ign wars exhausted SRI LANKA'S energies. After his reign had ended northern Sri Lanka was invaded by the Tamils and its capital was moved further and further south to reach Kotte (near Colombo) in the 1500s.

Sailendra (Kings of the Mountain), the Javanese dynasty that built BOROBUDUR, lost Java but took over SRIVIJAYA by the mid-800s.

Sri Lanka, an island off the coast of India which used to be called Ceylon, was a flourishing Buddhist civilization centred on the northern capital of Anuradhapura. About 1001-04 the Chola King Rajaraja I invaded from India and brought Hinduism with him. The Sri Lankans then moved their capital south to Polonnaruwa until King Parakrama Bahu I drove out the Cholas. He also restored the irrigation system that had been built by Mahasen, a heretical king reigning in the 300s.

Srivijaya, based on Palembang, southern Sumatra, profited in the 600s from Arab-Chinese trade. By 775 it controlled the waters around Sumatra and had annexed Kedah, Kelantan, Pahang and Trengganu in Malaya. But by the mid-800s, a SAILENDRA king from Java had taken over Srivijaya. The empire went into slow decline after several Chola attacks began from southern India in 1031.

Sultanate of Delhi (1211-1526) was set up following the conquests of Qutb ud-din Aibak in the 1190s. Qutb assumed power in Lahore in 1206, but was killed playing *chaugan* (a game similar to polo) in 1210, a year before the Sultanate came into being.

Thai people had lived near the Yangtse Kiang for 600 years before they began to muster their forces around AD 100. Then they moved south to form the kingdoms of Sukhothai (about 1238), Chiang Mai (later 1200s), Laos and Siam (by about 1350). When the Burmese kingdom of Pagan collapsed in 1287, the Thai were encouraged to expand further by KUBLAI KHAN (*see page 27*). In 1431 they sacked ANGKOR, and set up their capital at Ayuthaya.

Iron Pillar of Delhi

White Huns may have been a fair-skinned branch of the Yueh-chih who set up the Kushan kingdom in India about AD 80.

Muhammad's teachings and the *Arabian Nights* of the Caliph of Baghdad lie at opposite ends of the Islamic cultural spectrum. What is often forgotten is the great Arab contribution to medicine, the physical sciences and literature.

The Arabs

The outside world knew little about the Arabs until the 600s, when, fired with the fervour of their new religion of Islam, they swept out of the sand deserts of Arabia into the more fertile regions of Asia, Africa and Europe. Within a century, they conquered and converted to Islam an area larger than the old Roman empire. They absorbed the learning of the ancient world, and later passed it on to the Europeans. They evolved unique styles of ART and for several centuries led the Western world in cultural attainment. The Arab-Islamic civilization began dramatically in 622 as the result of a single incident in the life of one man – Muhammad (570–632).

Muhammad – a prophet from the desert

Muhammad, an orphan, was brought up by his relatives in Mecca, a wealthy town standing at the crossroads of the Arabian trade routes, and a centre of religious pilgrimage. The Arabs of that time worshipped the moon, many idols, and certain stones. The most sacred of these was the Black Stone, housed in the Kaaba, a large, cube-shaped building in Mecca. But not all visitors to Mecca worshipped the Black Stone. Some were Jews, Christians or MANDAEANS and the many religious arguments that Muhammad heard made a deep impression on him.

At the age of 25, Muhammad took employment as caravan manager to Khadija, a wealthy widow of 40 whom he later married. Muhammad began to have visions in which he claimed that Allah spoke to him, and gradually he evolved a new faith, *Islam* (Submission). Its demands were simple: give up the worship of idols and stones and submit to the one God, Allah.

Few supported Muhammad beyond close relatives, some slaves, and a merchant named Abu Bakr, because most Meccans saw their profits bound up with the continuance of the pilgrimages to the Kaaba. They believed that Muhammad's activities threatened their livelihood, and one night civic leaders sent soldiers to arrest him. Muhammad escaped in the darkness accompanied by Abu Bakr. The Meccans put a price of 100 camels on Muhammad's head, but did not catch him. His flight from Mecca – the Hegira (622) – is the most important event in Islam's history. From it dates the MUSLIM ERA.

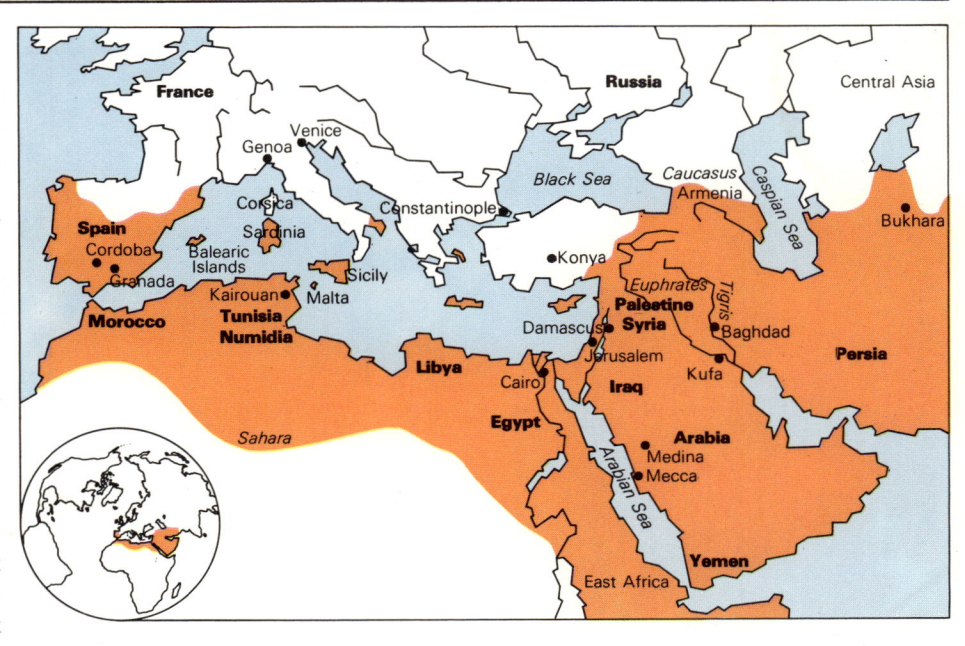

Above: Emerging from the Arabian desert in AD 632, the Muslims won a great empire. The map shows the empire's extent in 945.

Above: The bustling spice market in Cairo still retains the character of the past.

A triumphal return to Mecca

Muhammad and Abu Bakr first hid in a cave, then travelled on camel-back 300 kilometres north to the rival trading town of Medina. Word had gone before and the Medinans accepted Muhammad's new religion and made him their ruler. In 630, Muhammad rode back in triumph to Mecca at the head of an army. He smashed the idols in the Kaaba but, by sparing the Black Stone, won the Meccans for Islam.

When Muhammad died in 632, most of Arabia

Reference

Abbasid family descended from Abbas, uncle of Muhammad. In 750 the head of the family, Abu-L-Abbas, became the first of 37 Abbasid caliphs ruling mainly from Baghdad.

Abd al-Rahman (731-88), a boy of 20 when the Abbasids murdered his UMMAYAD relatives, swam the Euphrates to escape the killers. His brother turned back, and was murdered. Destitute, Abd al-Rahman wandered for 5 years as a fugitive before reaching Spain, where he re-founded the Umayyad dynasty.

Alcohol, strictly forbidden by Muhammad and the Arabian caliphs, was illegally enjoyed by the easier-going citizens of Damascus and Baghdad. Jews and Christians became the 'bootleggers' of the times.

Ali (c. 600–61) expected to become caliph at the death of Muhammad (his father-in-law), but Umar arranged the accession of Abu Bakr instead. Ali eventually became fourth caliph in 656, but was assassinated by the Kaharijites, an extreme Muslim sect. His death divided Islam.

Al-Kindi (c.800s), primarily a philosopher who interpreted Aristotle, wrote some 265 works on an immense number of topics. He attacked alchemy and miracles.

Gardens of Alhambra palace

Arab travellers included Ibn Batuta, who left Morocco on the HAJJ to Mecca in 1325. Travel so inspired him that he went on for another 120,000 km into Yemen, East Africa, Persia, India, Sri Lanka, Sumatra, China, central Asia and Siberia. Later, he crossed the Sahara into the kingdoms of Mali and Songhai. His accounts reveal otherwise unknown aspects of history.

Arabian Nights, originally a collection of tales from several countries, especially India, were 'arabized' in Baghdad and set amid the

The Arabs

Below: The *mihrab*, a niche in the mosque wall, must be accurately positioned. By facing it when they pray, Muslims can be sure that they are also facing Mecca. The *mihrab* shown is in the solidly-constructed Hassan mosque built in Cairo by the Mamluke rulers of Egypt in the mid-1300s.

Right: Beautifully-illustrated Korans became one of the main features of Arab art. Because Muhammed disapproved of portraying humans and animals, Muslim artists set their talents to devising pleasing geometrical designs and superb calligraphy, such as is shown on this double page from a Koran.

had been conquered for Islam. Mecca became the main religious centre, while Medina remained the hub of political affairs.

The caliphs of Mecca

At Muhammad's death, the faithful Abu Bakr was elected caliph (successor). Humble as ever, he continued to sell his cloth in the market place of Medina, while his army commanders began a *jihad* (holy war) in his name against the Byzantines in Syria. Abu Bakr outlived Muhammad by only two years. Umar, an early convert who had at one time persecuted Muhammad, succeeded him (634–44), and was in turn followed by Uthman, Muhammad's elderly son-in-law (644–56). Both men met death at the hands of assassins.

Uthman's killers appointed ALI, also a son-in-law of Muhammad, as fourth caliph (651–61), but many took up arms against him, including AYESHA, one of Muhammad's widows. Eventually, Ali took her captive on a battlefield where more than 12,000 Muslims lay dead. After five years as caliph, Ali too, was assassinated. The caliphate at first passed to his son HASAN, but Ali's sworn enemy, Muawiya, forced him to abdicate and founded the UMAYYAD dynasty, which ruled from Damascus 661–750.

The Umayyads in Damascus

Damascus had been a Roman-Byzantine city for 700 years, and in Muawiya's time it took on a lively character that remained largely unchanged into the present century. Baggy-trousered turbanned merchants jostled in the narrow market streets with loose-gowned Bedouin from Arabia.

court of Harun al-Rashid (c.764–809).

Architecture of merit barely existed in Muhammad's time. In spirit, the Arabs lived as tent-dwelling nomads. Their conquests changed this, and they took over the temples and churches of conquered peoples and turned them into mosques. Their own buildings usually followed local architectural styles and they had no desire to compete with the Byzantine grandeur. They thought rather that mosques should be simple houses of prayer. When churches or Zoroastrian fire temples became mosques, structural changes had to be made. Christians faced eastwards to the altar; Muslims southwards to Mecca. In newly built towns, early mosques were extremely simple, and at Kufa, in Iraq, the Muslims merely enclosed a square of land by a ditch. Then they built a *zulla*, or covered colonnade, from the marble of ruined buildings along the side nearest to Mecca to protect worshippers from the burning sun. Within half a century, Islam lost its simplicity and the Dome of the Rock in Jerusalem (built 687–91) and the Umayyad mosque in Damascus (completed 715) borrowed much from the Byzantine style. The Muslims also built great citadels which influenced castle architecture in Europe by way of the CRUSADES.

Golden Friday mosque, Baghdad

Art in the Arab world centres mainly around the mosque. It includes glassmaking, metal working, ceramic tilework, plasterwork, textiles, wood carving, carpet and rug making, book illustration, book binding and calligraphy. Muhammad banned idols and images, which led to an absence of sculpture and of the representation of humans and animals in paintings.

Assassins belonged to the Ismaili sect. The name came from *hashish*, the drug under whose influence they carried out sacred murders.

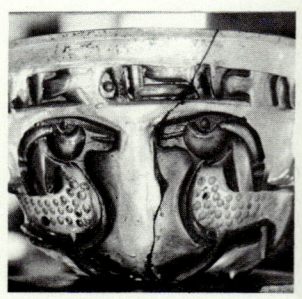

Early Arabic glass

The Arabs

Veiled women peeped through high latticed windows into the traffic below where sherbert and sweetmeat vendors called their wares above the din. Harassed men whipped donkeys and camels into the bazaars, rich with the smell of spices, perfumes and foodstuffs. The rooms of private houses surrounded courtyards in which stood fountains connected to the city's water supply.

Class structure

Below the caliph and his household were four classes: the Arabian Muslims; newly-converted Muslims; *dhimmis* (Jews, Christians and Mandaeans); and SLAVES. The converts included mainly Jews, Byzantines, Syrians, Persians and Egyptians, who quickly adopted Arab ways, but had a higher cultural level than the true Arabs. They eagerly married Arabs, served in the government, and became the most fanatical Muslims. The dhimmis enjoyed considerably more freedom than the slaves, who came mostly from Spain, Africa and central Asia.

The converts led the way in Arab medicine, philosophy, mathematics, science, art, literature and even language. Because of their origins, they borrowed heavily from higher civilizations. Converts rebuilt the Christian Basilica of St John in Damascus (originally a temple to Jupiter), which became the magnificent Umayyad mosque.

The caliphs of Damascus and Baghdad

In Damascus, the stark puritanism of the desert Muslims seemed out of place. The easy-going Caliph Muawiya married a Christian, appointed non-Muslims to government posts, and honoured poets, a group abhorred and banned by Muhammad. The Umayyad court enjoyed music, song, gambling and drinking. Successive caliphs became more and more worldly, and Hisham (reigned 724–43) neglected the empire for horseracing. His nephew Walid, who inherited an empire extending from Morocco to Mongolia, was atheistic, proud and talented, but incompetent. The Damascus mob cut off his head in 744, and paraded it through the streets on a spear.

The Umayyads tottered on for another six years, until the rival ABBASID FAMILY mustered a large army in Persia, where people still mourned the murder of Ali. They attacked in alliance with a breakaway sect called the SHI'ITES. In remembrance of Ali, the Abbasids and Shi'ites draped their soldiers, horses and camels in black, and

Above: The black-draped Kaaba in Mecca, the holiest shrine in Islam, was a centre of worship long before the time of Muhammad. It houses the sacred Black Stone. Muslims from every part of the world are expected to visit the Kaaba once in their lifetime. They are then respected as *hajjis* or pilgrims.

Left: Oases were the settled homes of the early Arabs and the halting places for desert traders and nomads. The essential thing that an oasis must have is water. The picture shows Nefta, an oasis of south-western Tunisia that grew into a town. Islam spread through the desert from oasis to oasis before it was established in the cities of the Mediterranean hinterland.

Hasan Sabbah founded the order of Assassins about 1090, from a mountain top south of the Caspian Sea.

Astrolabes, used to measure altitudes, positions and movements of heavenly bodies, became the main instrument of navigation until the invention of the sextant in the 1700s.

Avicenna or Ibn Sina (980–1037) was a converted Arab physician-philosopher born near Bukhara. His views led the field in world medicine 1100-1500.

Ayesha (died 678), daughter of Abu Bakr, married Muhammad when she was 9 and he was 52. About the same time, Muhammad's 15-year-old daughter, Fatima, married ALI. Ayesha opposed Ali's appointment as caliph in 656, raised Iraq to revolt and fought him until he captured her.

Baghdad, on the Tigris, was founded by Mansur, second ABBASID caliph, in 762 and its population reached 2 million. It was destroyed by Mongols in 1258 and 1400, and again by Persians in 1524.

Berbers have lived in north-western Africa since prehistory, and their culture has been traced back to 2400 BC. Many were Jews or Christians before they became Muslims.

Circassians came from the Black Sea-Caucasus area (now south-western USSR).

Crusades. The First Crusade (1096–99) began at the urging of Pope Urban II (c.1042–99), who responded to an appeal from the emperor of Constantinople to free Palestine from the Seljuk Turks. The Crusaders (mainly Franks) took Jerusalem in 1099. The Second Crusade (1147–49), led by Franks and Germans, ended in a Muslim victory.

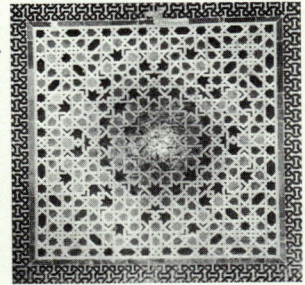

Arab tilework

The Third Crusade (1189–92), led by the French, German and English kings, failed to recapture Jerusalem from SALADIN. In the Fourth Crusade (1202–04) penniless Crusaders stranded in Venice struck a bargain with the Venetians to ship them to the eastern Mediterranean. In return they joined forces and plundered wealthy Constantinople. They deposed the Byzantine emperor and installed Baldwin of Flanders as first of the Latin emperors who ruled from Constantinople 1204–61. A Children's

The Arabs

Left: Granada, one of the showpieces of the Arab world, was the last part of Spain to be lost by the Arabs. The splendid Court of Lions in the dream-like Alhambra palace in Granada city, incorporates the finest features of Arab architecture. It took 200 years to build and was completed shortly before all Spain was lost to the Christians.

flew black banners. West of the Tigris they defeated the Umayyads in a terrible nine-days' battle and swept into Damascus. Then, by a trick, they murdered almost the entire Umayyad family and set up the Abbasid caliphate in the SUNNITE tradition. The second Abbasid caliph transferred the capital to the new city of BAGHDAD, and for the next 500 years nearby PERSIA dominated the character of Islam.

By the reign of Harun al-Rashid, fabled caliph of the ARABIAN NIGHTS, Baghdad became one of the world's most splendid cities and the caliph's luxurious palace, rising to a height of 40 metres over the audience chamber, boasted the costliest furnishings in Asia. Harun's cousin-wife, Zubaydal, studded her shoes with gems. Musicians, poets, and other worldly guests of the royal pair ate sumptuous food from gold and silver containers ornamented with jewels. The wealthy merchants of Baghdad took to drinking ALCOHOL, and spent much of their time at the public baths or at sports meetings.

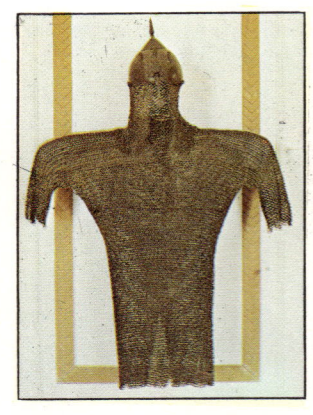

Above: A Mamluke soldier wore this coat of mail in the early 1300s. The Mamlukes twice halted foreign invaders when all other Arab resistance had failed.

Trade and translation

The Muslims first turned to seafaring in Muawiya's time and under the Abbasids, Arab and Persian ships laden with drugs, gems, pearls and spices sailed to Tang dynasty China and brought back bronze mirrors, ironware, porcelain, silks and tea. The wharves of Baghdad's port on the Tigris extended for several kilometres, and their warehouses held a hundred imports from Arabia, Egypt, Africa, Syria, Persia, central Asia, India, Malaya, China, Russia and Scandinavia. The Arabs traded along overland camel routes. Their Arab ships did not use the square sail of the Europeans, but the *lateen*, a tall triangular sail that caught the wind on either side, yet kept the same edge forward. Diplomacy followed in the wake of trade. But an Arab envoy to the court of China ruffled court etiquette by refusing to kowtow to the Tang emperor, saying that he bowed only to Allah.

The Abbasids grew hungry for learning and promoted translations into Arabic from Greek, Persian, Sanskrit and Syrian works of science and philosophy. Gradually, Arabic became the language of all learned people from Spain to central Asia. While the Frank emperor Charlemagne (*see page 24*) could just write his name, Harun al-Rashid studied translations of complex works. Through Arab scholars, the forgotten learning of the ancient world eventually found its way into the Latin books of medieval Europe.

Culture and science in Baghdad

By 850, Arab scholarship flourished in its own right. Textbooks on medicine were written by RHAZES and AVICENNA, and AL-KINDI wrote some 265 works on subjects ranging from optics to music. The Arabs were interested in more than the theory of medicine, and established pharmacies, hospitals and rural clinics.

Learning from India, Arab astronomers made regular observations with accurate instruments by the 900s and built observatories near Baghdad and Damascus. Using the ASTROLABE, dial, globe and quadrant, the caliph's astronomer measured the length of a degree of the

---

Crusade (1212) resulted in the death or enslavement of 50,000 children before they left Europe. There were several further Crusades, lasting into the 1400s, but these were not of great importance.

E **Emir,** a title given to Arab chieftains, is especially connected with the supposed descendants of Muhammad's daughter, FATIMA.

F **Fatima** (606–32) daughter of Muhammad and Khadija, married ALI.

Fatimite (or Fatimid) dynasty claimed descent from Fatima. Between the 900s and the 1100s, they occupied at various times, Tunisia, Sicily, Algeria, Libya, Malta, Sardinia, Corsica, Balearic Islands, Genoa, Egypt, Palestine and Syria. The Fatimite dynasty ended when SALADIN took Egypt in 1170.

G **Granada** became capital city of the kingdom of Granada, the last Spanish region held by the Moors, in 1238. It fell to the Christians in 1492. The city contains the Alhambra, the Moorish citadel and palace.

H **Hajj** (pilgrimage to Mecca) is commanded by the Koran, and millions make the journey every year. Hajji walk 7 times around the Kaaba and kiss the sacred Black Stone while wearing only unsewn clothes. They usually also visit the Muhammad mosque at Medina and the pilgrimage ends with Id al-Adha, a feast at which healthy sheep, goats or camels are sacrificed, and their meat given to the poor.

Hasan, son of ALI and grandson of Muhammad, abdicated as fifth caliph in 661 under pressure from the UMAYYADS. The SHI'ITES believed that the Umayyads poisoned Hasan. He and Ali are the two chief Shi'ite martyrs.

Masyaf Castle, near Hama, Syria

I **Iberians** settled in Spain before 600 BC, probably coming from Africa.

Iman is the faith in Allah and in his prophet, Muhammad, that all Muslims must have. It is also the name given to the priest of a mosque.

J **Jerusalem,** already sacred to Jews and Christians, was also favoured by the early Muslims. They believed that

earth's circumference to within one per cent of accuracy. One of the astronomer-mathematicians about 1100 was UMAR KHAYYAM better known in his role as the free-thinking Persian poet.

The Arabs also pioneered alchemy and chemistry, using the experimental method rather than the inadequate philosophical approach of the Greeks. Arab research proved fairly accurate, and was based on the patient collection and analysis of fact. Their weakness lay in failing to project hypotheses from which they could draw scientifically-based conclusions.

Arab geography and Muslim law
The religious obligation for Muslims to make the HAJJ (pilgrimage) to Mecca, and to position the MIHRAB in mosques so that worshippers faced Mecca, inspired the study of geography. Al-Masudi, one of many intrepid ARAB TRAVELLERS, visited places as far apart as Madagascar, Sri Lanka and China, questioning peoples of different religions and recording his findings.

Astrology also promoted geography, because astrologers needed to determine latitudes and longitudes. Using a translation of PTOLEMY'S GEOGRAPHY, some 70 scholars, led by a mathematician called Khwarizmi (780–c.850), constructed a vast map of the earth and sky. But although Muslim merchants found their way into Africa, China and Russia, they feared to venture into the 'Sea of Darkness': the Atlantic.

Below: A Crusader knight engages in a fight to the death with his Saracen counterpart in one of the many bloody battles for possession of the 'Holy Land' of Palestine and Syria. 'Saracen' became the general term for all those Muslims who fought the Crusaders.

Muhammad ascended to heaven from there, at the spot where a rock now protrudes through the Dome of the Rock. Muhammad at first prayed towards Jerusalem; only later towards the Kaaba in Mecca. The city is still sacred to the 3 religions.

M**Mamlukes** (in Arabic, *slaves*), were originally Turks, Mongols and CIRCASSIANS enslaved by the Arabs. The caliphs of Egypt used them as soldiers, but they came to dominate their 'masters' and from 1250 became sultans of Egypt. Ottoman Turks ended their dynasty in 1517, but the Mamlukes kept most of their power until 1811.
Mandaeans (or Sabians), a sect from Persia, held beliefs similar to the Zoroastrians, Magi, and Babylonian astrologers. They honoured St John the Baptist because they believed in ritual bathing, although they baptized long before St John's time. Mandaeans still practise their religion in Iran and Iraq, and their holy book is the *Ginza Rba*.
Marrakesh, the south-western centre of Muslim trade and culture, was the Moroccan capital 1062–1259.
Mihrab, a niche in the

Mosque in Tinerhir, Morocco

mosque wall, is the place where an IMAN leads the Muslims in prayer. Because they must face Mecca when praying, the positioning of the *mihrab* is crucial.
Muslim era dates from the Hegira, Muhammad's flight from Mecca to Medina in 622. AH is used before Muslim years, just as AD is used in front of Christian years. Following the moon rather than the sun, the Arabs had 12 months alternately of 29 or 30 days in length, giving a 354-day year. The Muslim year is therefore 11.25 days short of the solar year of the Christians.
Muslim law (Sharia) is a combined and complex system of civil and criminal law and social and religious behaviour, still used by Islamic countries. It is based on the *Revelations,* words of God revealed to Muhammad and recorded in the Koran, and *Hadith* (tradition). *Hadith* is the teachings of Muhammad not directly revealed by God and not included in the Koran.
Muslim-Christian clashes encouraged the Christians to consider an alliance with the

Left: Arab trading boats such as the one shown became a familiar sight in the Mediterranean and Arabian seas from the time of the Umayyad caliphate onwards. Later, Arab seamen sailed eastwards to India and China.

Right: The astrolabe, a navigational instrument probably invented by the Babylonians, remained vital to seamen for well over 2,000 years. This Arab astrolabe was made by a master craftsmen over 1,000 years ago.

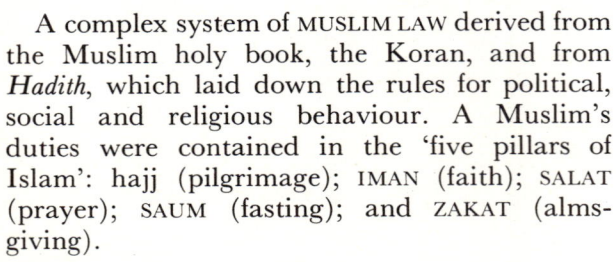

A complex system of MUSLIM LAW derived from the Muslim holy book, the Koran, and from *Hadith*, which laid down the rules for political, social and religious behaviour. A Muslim's duties were contained in the 'five pillars of Islam': hajj (pilgrimage); IMAN (faith); SALAT (prayer); SAUM (fasting); and ZAKAT (almsgiving).

Umayyad Spain

Not all the Umayyads died in 750. One, ABD AL-RAHMAN, fled westwards and became EMIR of Spain (756–88). He transformed Spain into a land of spacious cities laid out with gardens and strove hard to weld the various peoples of the country, Arabs, BERBERS, Goths, IBERIANS, NUMIDIANS and Syrians, into one nation.

Abd al-Rahman chose for his capital the ancient city of Cordoba, where he built a palace with gardens and the Great Mosque, all in the Syrian style. He also built hundreds of smaller mosques, baths, and an aqueduct to supply the city with pure water. Cordoba soon grew to a city of 500,000 surpassed in culture only by Constantinople and Baghdad. In 929, Abd al-Rahman III (891–961) took the title caliph in opposition to the ABBASID FAMILY.

Industry and trade boomed in Umayyad Spain. The cordwainers (leather workers) especially, were world-famed. The country also excelled in agricultural science, especially fruit-growing. The 'hard currency' coinage of Umayyad Spain passed freely throughout the Christian countries to the north. Cordoba became the centre of learning, and its university, founded in the 900s, was known all over the world. The caliph Al-Harun is said to have accumulated 400,000 books, more than 20 times as many books as then existed in Christian Europe.

North Africa

All North Africa fell to the Arabs in the 600s. At first, the Egyptians remained Coptic Christians, but later most converted to Islam to secure social and financial advantages. Arab migration into Egypt played an important part in forming the country's culture and religion.

Kairouan in Tunisia, founded as a sacred city in 670, became the capital of the Arab FATIMITE dynasty in 909. This dynasty, founded by Ubaidullah, claimed descent from Muhammad's daughter, FATIMA. From Tunisia, the Fatimites took Libya and Egypt, founded Cairo in 969 and the Al-Azhar mosque and university in 970. Their dynasty lasted 200 years before falling to SALADIN in 1171.

Mongols, and in 1245 the pope sent a Franciscan friar to the Great Khan in Mongolia. Louis IX of France followed suit and sent a Flemish missionary in 1253, but nothing came of either of these contacts.

Numidians came from Numidia, roughly present-day Algeria.

Persia destroyed by Alexander the Great, rose again in 226 under the dynasty of the Sassanids, who restored the Zoroastrian religion. In 260 the Sassanid emperor Shapur I (241–72) defeated the Roman emperor Valerian, who died in captivity. The Sassanids built an empire that at times extended into Syria, Armenia and Egypt. Sassanid Persia finally fell to the Arabs in 641–42, and replaced Zoroastrianism with Islam.

Ptolemy's Geography remained a standard work for 1,400 years after the Greco-Egyptian scientist produced it in about 127-41. The work had many errors because Ptolemy underestimated the earth's circumference.

Rhazes (c.860–c.925), chief physician at the Baghdad hospital, produced several textbooks on medicine. In one of these he distinguished between smallpox and measles. Europeans printed his textbooks in Latin translation 500 years after his death.

Saladin (or Salah-al-Din, 1138–93), a Kurd, took Egypt for the ABBASIDS, but in 1170 proclaimed himself sultan, so beginning the Ayyubite dynasty. He extended his territory into Tunisia, Yemen, Damascus and Jerusalem. A brilliant general who fought the Crusaders, Saladin was also a man of considerable culture.

Inscriptions in plaster, Alhambra

Salat (Muslim prayers) must be recited 5 times a day: at dawn, noon, afternoon, evening and nightfall. Desert Muslims prayed facing Mecca after washing in water; if there was none, they used sand.

Saum (fasting) is prescribed during Ramadan, the ninth month of the Muslim year, when Muslims may not eat, drink or smoke between sunrise and sunset. Travellers, sick people, nursing mothers, and soldiers on active service are exempt. Ramadan ends with the feast of Id al-Fitr.

In the 1000s the Almoravides (Muslim Berbers) seized Morocco for the Arabs, then took over Umayyad Spain. Another Berber dynasty, the Almohades, took over in Morocco and Spain in the 1170s.

Seljuks and Crusaders

Although the Abbasids never held Spain, and lost North Africa and Syria-Palestine to the Fatimites, the period 750-1055 proved to be a 'golden age'. This was followed by a series of troubles, beginning when the Seljuk Turks attacked from central Asia. In 1055, the Seljuk leader Tughril swept unopposed into Baghdad. Although he allowed the Abbasids to remain caliphs, Tughril dominated their empire as sultan. Further west, the tougher Fatimites successfully resisted the Seljuks, who set up their capital at Konya in Asia Minor, but in 1092 after the death of their strong sultan, Malik Shah, they split into factions.

By the late 1000s, several strong Christian kingdoms had been established which resented the Muslim occupation of Spain and Syria-Palestine, and consequently MUSLIM-CHRISTIAN CLASHES became frequent. The most important were the CRUSADES, fought about 1096-1291. The Crusaders took JERUSALEM in 1099, but SALADIN retook it for the Abbasids in 1187.

Mongols and Spanish Christians

The Abbasids' most terrible and final peril came when Genghiz Khan began the great Mongol expansion. Having conquered northern China, he and his successors rode westwards into Russia and central Europe. In 1258, Hulagu, grandson of Genghiz Khan, led the final assault that breached the walls of Baghdad. The Mongols poured into the starving city, murdered the caliph, his family and officials, massacred more than half of Baghdad's two million people, and razed the city to the ground. Plague inevitably broke out. Once again, effective resistance came from Egypt, since 1254 under the control of the MAMLUKES.

In Spain, the Christians pushed the declining Muslims ever southwards, and by 1276, only GRANADA remained Muslim. Although the great days of the Arabs were over, the Islamic religion continued to expand under foreign leadership.

Below: Baghdad's chequered history reached its climax in 1258, when Hulagu, grandson of Genghiz Khan, laid siege to the city with stone-slinging machines and flame throwers. The Mongols destroyed the city after its surrender, killed half of its 2 million inhabitants, and beat the caliph to death. Here Mongols and Arabs are seen in full battle.

Shi'ites (or Shiahs), supporters of ALI and his descendants, belong to the smaller of the 2 main divisions of Islam. Shi'ite sects include Ismailis, and their sub-sect ASSASSINS, FATIMITES and SUFIS.

Slaves of the Arabs numbered several millions of captives from different nations. Muslims could not enslave other Muslims, but slaves who converted to Islam remained slaves. Several slaves gained their freedom and attained high positions – even the caliphate. In Egypt slaves founded the successful MAMLUKE dynasty.

Sufis added ideas from Plato, Buddhism and Christianity to their SHI'ITE beliefs. UMAR KHAYYAM was one of several Sufi poets.

Sunnites are members of 4 Islamic sects (Hanifite, Malikite, Shafi'ite or Hanbalite) that follow the main tradition of Islam. 90 per cent of all Muslims are Sunnite. Apart from SHI'ITES, other sects include Ikwan (Wahabis) and Kharijites.

Gateway in Marrakesh

U Umar Khayyam (1000s), a Persian poet and scientist, became the outstanding mathematician of his time. His RUBAIYAT contains the famous lines (in translation) 'The Moving Finger writes, and having writ moves on...'

Umayyads, a family at first hostile to Muhammad, provided the third caliph, Uthman, Muhammad's son-in-law. The sixth caliph, Muawiya, made the caliphate hereditary, and was followed in Damascus by 13 other Umayyad caliphs.

Z Zakat (almsgiving) is both compulsory and voluntary for Muslims, who had to give some 2 per cent of the wealth they had held for a year. They were also expected to give alms beyond this amount.

Sand dunes in the Sahara

Charlemagne was the first of the Holy Roman emperors, crowned by Pope Leo III. In return for papal backing, he promoted church affairs and education. Many of the great European monasteries and monastic orders were founded by the Franks.

The Franks

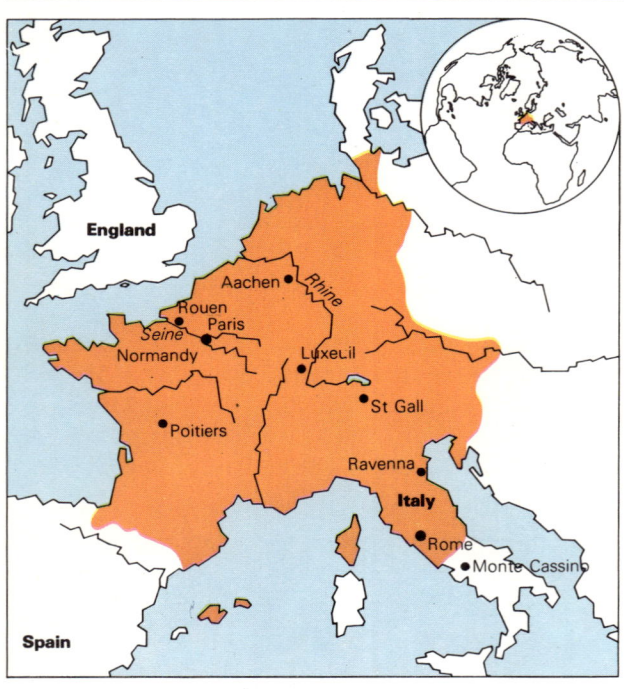

Left: Under Charlemagne, the kingdom of the Franks emerged as the successor to the Roman empire in the West. But culturally it proved no match for Byzantium, and its unity disappeared soon after Charlemagne's death.

The collapse of Rome signalled the rise to power of the Germanic Franks. Between 481 and 800 they built up a star-shaped empire with its 'points' in modern Spain, Normandy, Denmark, Hungary and Italy. It became the first truly European Christian empire and one of its important legacies was the establishment of many great MONASTERIES, centres of learning and art. Under Charlemagne (*see page 24*) the empire reached its peak and challenged Byzantium as heir to Rome.

The tribal empire

The Franks were the northernmost of the GERMANIC TRIBES attacking the old Roman frontiers, and by the 200s they had settled along the middle and lower Rhine River. The northern Franks allied themselves to Rome and moved southwards into Gaul. When the northern leader, CLOVIS I, united all the Franks into an orderly Christian empire, the pope readily supported him. Clovis established the Merovingian dynasty and reigned 481-511.

Frankish arts

The period of the Frankish empire before Charlemagne is often called the 'Dark Ages', but the arts flourished in north-west Europe. Information about them comes mainly from finds made in graves of the period; much jewellery as well as normal grave goods were based on Roman originals.

Frankish jewellery is very distinctive, the early forms copying late Roman belt buckles. Massive gold brooches are typical, often heavily set with garnets, ornamented with gold or silver filigree, and sometimes using late Roman gold coins as pendants. Particularly rich Frankish graves have been found at various places such as Cologne and outside Paris.

Right: This magnificent gold reliquary set with precious jewels is a fine example of the superior quality of Frankish art.

Reference

Aachen (Aix-la-Chapelle), probable birthplace of Charlemagne, became his main capital, where he built his palace and a splendid cathedral that houses his tomb. The cathedral was largely rebuilt in the 900s after NORSEMEN destroyed it.

Administrators. Charlemagne ruled as an autocrat aided by his favourites and religious and secular officials. Dukes or 'margraves' ruled groups of counties in border areas, and from 200–250 interior counties each came under the control of a count. Each bishop's diocese normally covered the same area as a county. From 802 the counties were gathered in groups of 6–10, each of which became a district inspected annually by Charlemagne's envoys. He also visited each district in turn himself until ill health prevented him from travelling.

Architecture and art of the Carolingians was a combination of Roman, Byzantine and German styles reflected particularly in the illustrated manuscripts and ivory and enamel work of the Frankish monks. Charlemagne's round palace church at Aachen was embellished by columns, mosaics and marble which Charlemagne ordered to be brought from Italy.

Capet, Hugh (reigned 987–96), fought the last Carolingian king to possess the French crown and found the Capetian dynasty.

Church affairs became a special interest of Charlemagne's. He arranged for the clergy to be educated, intervened in the appointment of bishops, and arbitrated in religious disputes.

Carolingian ivory plaque

Clovis I (465–511) a tribal chieftain, murdered his way to the leadership of the Salian (northern) Franks by 481. In 486 he finally ended Roman control over Gaul, and became a Christian in gratitude for victory over the Alemanni in 496.

Education was encouraged by Charlemagne, who set up schools to teach and train the clergy. His own palace was a centre of intellectual activity.

France as a kingdom dates from the signing of

The Franks

Above: While in Rome to act as judge over Pope Leo III's trial, Charlemagne was tricked by him. The pope put an emperor's crown on the unsuspecting king's head. In crowning him emperor of the West, the pope sought to enhance his own power and status.

The Merovingians

The Franks conquered several other Germanic tribes, and by the 700s their empire covered much of western Europe, but it was disunited into several kingdoms with shifting borders. Its main kingdoms were Neustria (roughly modern France); Austrasia (roughly Netherlands to southern Germany); and Burgundy (roughly eastern France to Switzerland). After 639, the Merovingians became known as 'the idle kings' because real power had passed to the mayors of the palace.

The popes continued to support the Franks, seeing through their power the best hope for the Church's survival through dangerous times. Their wisdom was confirmed in 732 when the energetic mayor Charles Martel (c.689–741) decisively defeated an invading Arab Muslim force near Poitiers. When Charles's son, Pepin the Short (reigned 751–68) deposed the last Merovingian king in 751, Pope Zacharias hastened to crown him first king of the Carolingian dynasty.

Charlemagne

Pepin's son, Charlemagne, expanded the empire to its greatest extent. On Christmas Day 800, Pope LEO III crowned him emperor of the West. Until Charlemagne, the Franks had lived in small self-sufficient communities which had existed since pre-Roman times, where money had virtually no value because little trade existed beyond barter. Charlemagne reimposed a centralized government from his capital at AACHEN in the north and gave land to nobles who worked as judges, ADMINISTRATORS and army commanders, instead of paying rent. Poorer people had to provide food for the court and labour for government projects. Charlemagne promoted the interests of the CHURCH, EDUCATION, ARCHITECTURE and ART.

In 843, Charlemagne's three grandsons split the empire between them. The western part, the kingdom of FRANCE, soon fell prey to the NORSEMEN whose raids were concentrated around the present day Normandy area. In 987, France fell to Hugh CAPET, whose descendants ruled the kingdom for 800 years, although when Capet took over it had shrunk to little more than the area around PARIS.

Right: The power of the Frankish empire lay in Charlemagne's own military leadership. At his death there was little left to sustain its strength.

---

the Treaty of Verdun in 843, when Charles II became king of the western Franks.

G **Germanic tribes** who were conquered by the Franks and had their lands annexed, included Alemanni, Bavarians, Burgundians, Lombards, Saxons and Thuringians.

L **Leo III** (pope 795–816) crowned Charlemagne emperor in 800 after he had restored Rome to the pope after a revolt. This gave a sacred seal to Charlemagne's position as emperor, initiating the idea of the divine right of kings bestowed by the pope.

M **Monasteries** existed before Christianity among the Buddhists and Jains. St Benedict (c.480–c.543) founder of the Benedictine order, probably founded European monasticism when he established the Monte Cassino monastery in about 529. He drew up rules apportioning a monk's day between worship, meditation, study and manual labour. Early Frankish monasteries were established in the 500s at Luxeuil and St Gall.

N **Norsemen** (Norwegian and Danish Vikings) became a serious threat to the Franks and Charlemagne built a fleet to stop them. However, his successors let the fleet fall into a state of disrepair, and from about 843 the Norsemen sailed up the Seine River to loot Rouen and Paris. They encamped at the mouth of the river, preventing trade, and thus seriously threatening the future of Western civilization until in 911 they moved into their own territory. This land had been ceded to the Norse leader Rollo (c.860–c.931) by the French king, Charles the Simple (879–929). As their land expanded, it became the duchy of Normandy and the Norsemen adopted the French language and laws, were converted to Christianity, and came to call themselves Normans.

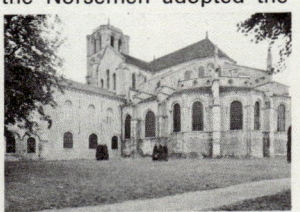

Vezelay Abbey, France

P **Paris** became the capital of CLOVIS I and several other Merovingian kings, after which it suffered looting and famine from Norse attacks. It recovered only after Hugh CAPET made it his capital.

The history of England from the collapse of the Roman empire to AD 1100 is one of invasion. First came the Jutes, Angles and Saxons, then the Vikings, and finally the Normans under William the Conqueror.

The English

Among the Germanic peoples set in movement by the collapse of the Roman empire were the JUTES, SAXONS AND ANGLES. They left their crowded homeland near the present-day Danish-German border, crossed the North Sea, and invaded southern Britain in about 450–550. Many of the native Britons fled to the west, where they preserved their Christian religion. By 827, the invaders had established the first permanent nation-state, which survived conquest by the Danes in 1013 and by the Normans in 1066.

Germanic invasions of Celtic Britain

Roman civilization soon fell into decay after 407 and organized government gave way to control by local Celtic chieftains. One, called Vortigern, is said to have invited two Jutish leaders, HENGEST AND HORSA, to land in Kent in 449 because he needed an ally against marauding Picts from the north.

The invaders avoided the crumbling towns and moved along river valleys or Roman roads. They settled in forest clearings off the main routes to avoid attack by the next wave of immigrants, and by 613, almost all present-day England was under their rule. The three tribes lost their separate identities and eventually became known as the Anglo-Saxons.

Northern and western Britain

In the 500s, the Angles extended their kingdom of Northumbria northwards to the Firth of Forth. To the west of them, refugee Britons set up the independent kingdom of Strathclyde. Then SCOTS crossed from Ireland to establish their own kingdom of Dalriada, north of Strathclyde, bringing with them their own form of Christianity. North of Northumbria, the warlike Picts had already established a southern kingdom and a northern kingdom and by the mid-700s they also dominated Dalriada and Strathclyde. However it was the culture of the Scots that survived in Dalriada and spread with the small groups who constantly migrated eastwards into the more fertile lands of the Picts and Angles, where their Gaelic language eventually replaced Pictish.

Some Britons became slaves of the Anglo-Saxons, while others integrated with them, often by marriage. Those who fled, set up kingdoms in

Right: Having united their 7 kingdoms into a loose confederation (the Heptarchy), the English later had to share England with the Danes. To the north of England (present-day Scotland), several kingdoms emerged.

Above: Alfred's jewel, bearing an inscription reading 'Alfred ordered me to be made', includes an enamel portrait of the king holding 2 sceptres.

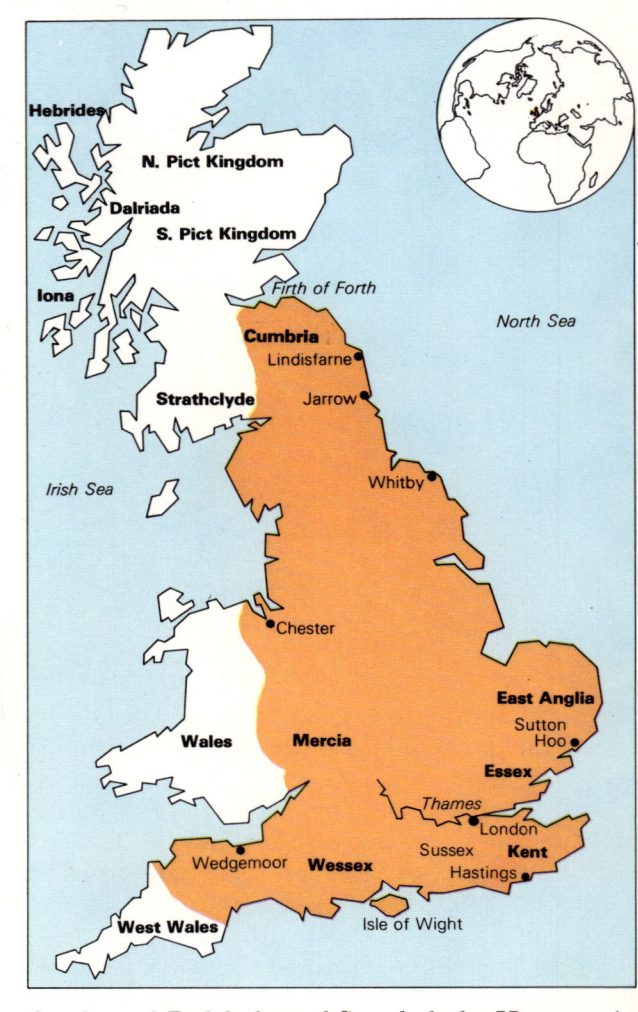

Reference

Alfred the Great, king of Wessex 871–99, had to divide England with the Danes. He revived English scholarship, and was himself a scholar.
Anglo-Saxon Chronicle recorded English history from early times to the 1100s.
Arthur (c.500s) traditionally lived in the west country. Although legend depicts him as a chivalrous king, records from a Welsh monastery of his own day, establish him not as a king but as a great British warrior.
Augustine, St. (c.600s) led missionaries from Rome into Kent in 597, where its Jutish king, Ethelbert, accepted Christianity and made Augustine the first Archbishop of Canterbury.

Beowulf is the epic story of a warrior-king who fought dragons and monsters, eventually losing his life to protect his people.

Caedmon, author of the *Hymn*, probably composed several other religious poems and influenced other poets.
Celtic Christians. St Ninian, a Briton appointed bishop by the pope, preached Christianity to the Southern Picts before 400, and St Patrick came from Rome to convert Ireland in 432. In 563, St Columba of Ireland founded a monastery on the island of Iona, and converted the Northern Picts. In turn, St Aidan and others from Iona founded a monastery at Lindisfarne, the Holy Island, in Northumbria. From there they converted kingdoms southwards to Mercia.
Cumbria, a Briton territory, lay south of and joined Strathclyde.

Tintagel – King Arthur's castle

Danelaw was roughly the land north-east of a line from London to Chester, extending almost to the present Scottish border. The Norman conquest brought about its end.

Harold II (c.1022–66) ruled for only 9 months in 1066 and was defeated and killed at the battle of Hastings.
Hengist and Horsa (according to Bede) quarrelled with and defeated Vortigern about 455, when Horsa was killed and Hengist formed the kingdom of Kent.

The English

Below: Anglo-Saxon warriors, displaced by the collapse of the 'Pax Romana', put to sea from the region of north Germany and Denmark and easily took southern Britain from the Romanized Celts. As Anglo-Saxon civilization developed, it came under increasing attack from the last warrior-migrants – the Vikings.

Right: High quality Anglo-Saxon metalworking came to light in 1939, when a great treasure, mostly gold, was found at Sutton Hoo, Suffolk, England. The objects found in a 25-metre longship in an East Anglian king's burial mound included the helmet and shoulder clasp shown. Many other objects were of gold, or were jewelled.

CUMBRIA, WALES, and WEST WALES. A semi-legendary British warrior, ARTHUR, is said to have fought against the Anglo-Saxons in the 500s.

Seven Anglo-Saxon kingdoms developed by 600: East Anglia, Essex, Kent, Sussex, Mercia, Northumbria and Wessex. The last three soon came to dominate the whole country, and fought each other for supremacy for two hundred years.

Religion and the arts

The Anglo-Saxons brought the old Germanic NATURE GODS with them into Britain, especially Odin (Woden) and Thor, and destroyed Christianity wherever they settled. However, the CELTIC CHRISTIANS spread their religion throughout present-day Ireland, Scotland and northern England. In 597, Saint AUGUSTINE of Rome landed in Kent and converted its people to Christianity. From there, Roman monks converted East Anglia, Sussex and Wessex. For a while, the Celtic and Roman forms of Christianity competed, but at the Synod of Whitby in 664, the Celtic Christians accepted the authority of Rome.

Early Anglo-Saxon literature included the *Hymn* of CAEDMON, composed in the 600s. About 100 years later, an unknown author composed the epic BEOWULF. At Jarrow, the VENERABLE BEDE (673–735) wrote the *Ecclesiastical History of the English People*.

The unification of England

While the Anglo-Saxon kings warred against each other, Viking attacks began, but by 828 King Egbert of Wessex (c.775–839) claimed to be king of all England. Welsh unity came about the same time, but did not last. In 850–70, Danish VIKINGS conquered all England except Wessex. King ALFRED of Wessex fought them constantly, but in 886 he signed the Treaty of Wedgemore with Guthrum the Danish leader. The Danes accepted Christianity and agreed to live in a vast area called the DANELAW. In 1016–35, King Canute of Denmark (c.994–1035) ruled all England, but his Anglo-Scandinavian empire collapsed at his death. The last Vikings to arrive landed from Normandy. The Normans defeated the last Saxon king, HAROLD II, at Hastings and brought all England under the iron rule of WILLIAM THE CONQUEROR in 1066.

J Jutes, Angles and Saxons occupied southern Britain by 613. The Jutes took Kent, the Isle of Wight, and the mainland opposite to it. The Saxons settled around the Thames River and pushed westwards to the Irish Sea. The Angles settled in central southern Britain and the eastern coastlands.

N Nature gods of the Anglo-Saxons included the sun and moon and Odin (Woden) and Thor, after whom Wednesday and Thursday are named.

O Offa's Dyke was an earthwork built on the Welsh border by King Offa of Mercia (757–96).

S Scots. King Kenneth MacAlpin of Dalriada (c.800s) claimed all the mainland north of the Firth of Forth as his kingdom of Scotland by 843. By 1034, Duncan I (c.1000s) ruled all Scotland.

T Three field system meant that 1 field was kept fallow, another sown to wheat or some other cereal, and a third was allocated to barley. In Anglo-Saxon villages they were cut into equal-sized strips and each family had strips distributed over the three fields.

V Venerable Bede, a great scholar, compiled an accurate history which influenced all western Europe.

Vikings from Denmark raided southern Britain, and those from Norway attacked northern Britain and Ireland. They pillaged isolated coasts and took slaves, settling in the Hebrides, Orkneys and Shetlands.

W Wales, never conquered by the Anglo-Saxons, was bordered by OFFA'S DYKE. The Welsh became semi-nomadic, keeping their own Celtic law, language and form of Christianity.

West Wales was the name for Cornwall and part of Devon.

William the Conqueror (1027–87) married Matilda, Duke of Flanders' daughter, a descendant of King ALFRED. He was promised the throne of England by HAROLD II while the latter was still a duke, and invaded when Harold pronounced himself king, defeating him at Hastings in 1066.

William on the Bayeux tapestry

The Vikings were expert sailors who used their seafaring skill to become pirates and coastal raiders. A Norwegian explorer, Leif Ericsson, may well have been the first European to discover America.

The Vikings

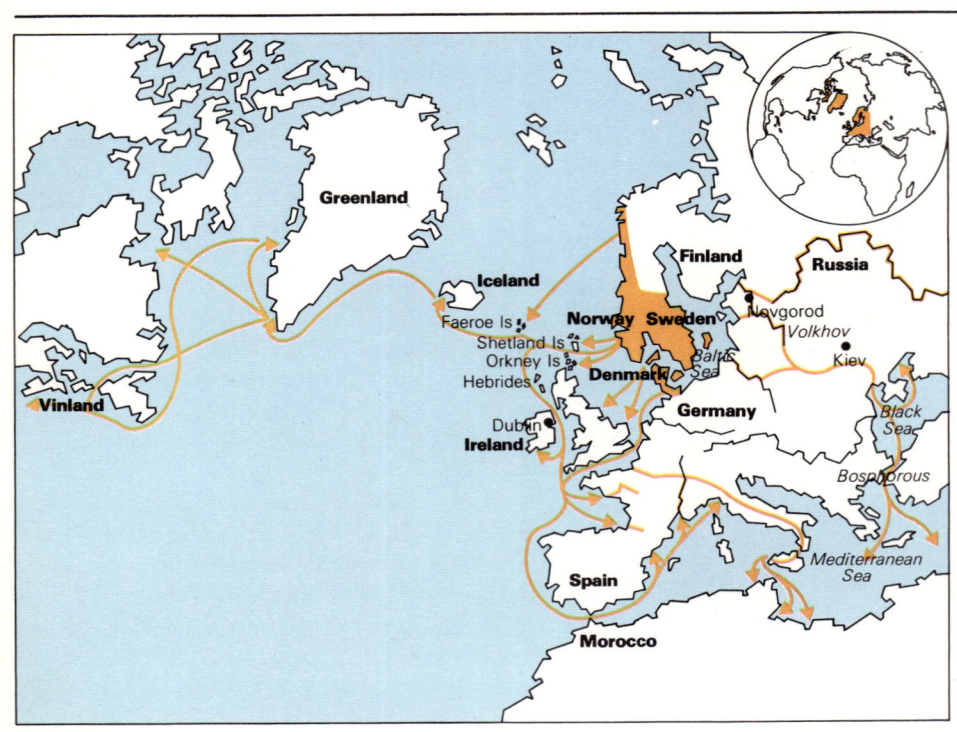

The Norsemen lived in Denmark and other colder lands of Norway and Sweden. Their own name for themselves was Vikings (men of the *viks* or creeks). They took to the sea in the 700s, seeking wealth through piracy and coastal raiding. They were probably forced to set sail because the climate in their homelands worsened, so reducing the productivity of their land. By contrast, the countries they raided seemed more attractive for settlement. Expert at shipbuilding, they became the most daring seamen Europe had ever known. Viking LONGSHIPS penetrated the seas and waterways of Europe and pioneered the route to North America.

Above: The Vikings put to sea first as pirates, later as settlers. Danes raided England, France and the Mediterranean; Swedes invaded Germany and Russia down to Constantinople; Norwegians braved the bleak Atlantic westwards to Iceland, Greenland and the coast of America.

The Vikings at home and abroad

Viking voyages were seasonal. At home, they planted crops in the spring before beginning their expeditions, and returned in summer to harvest them. Then they put to sea again, to return in winter before the sea became too dangerous. Ashore, they processed salt, tar and fish and made tools and weapons.

The Vikings built their long, shallow ships, sometimes as long as 100 metres, but typically 20 metres in length by five metres in width. These carried about 90 men. Oarsmen rowed the ships until they were out at sea, when they hoisted a single square sail. Using a steering oar (the early form of a rudder) they boldly set course to destinations mostly unknown to earlier seamen.

At sea, the Vikings were unbeatable, but they avoided battles on land, landing instead in force at lonely points to steal harvests, plunder rich monasteries, and seize monks and nuns as slaves. They struck silently and speedily after hiding their boats and those who survived their raids often starved to death.

The Vikings gained an evil reputation for needlessly killing, burning and destroying, but with more experience on land they proved highly adaptable to different circumstances. For example, if they landed where horses were to be found, they soon learned to ride them skilfully. Becoming bolder, they attacked and captured walled towns, improved their fortifications, then used them as bases from which to found permanent settlements. Once settled they prepared to repel the next wave of Vikings. Like the Anglo-Saxons before them, they gradually abandoned Odin and THOR, forgot their MYTHS, and accepted Christianity. In general, the Danes advanced to the south; the Swedes to the south-east; and the Norwegians to the far west.

The Danes and the Swedes

The main Danish attacks were made against the Franks and the English, and their efforts led to

Reference

B **Brian Boru** became king of Munster (southern Ireland) about 976, and High King of Ireland 1002–14. His reign marked an Irish 'golden age' and in 1014 he finally defeated the Danes at Clontarf (now part of Dublin) but he was killed in the battle.

D **Dublin** was built by Irish settlers in the 800s as a market centre from which they could exchange slaves and furs for silver and luxuries from the European mainland.

G **Germany** became a confederation in 962, when the pope crowned the duke of Saxony, Otto the Great, first Holy Roman Emperor. His crowning in Aachen signified that he was the 'new Charlemagne'. The Holy Roman emperors ruled until 1806.

Greenland, known to the Irish, was discovered by Eric the Red, a Norwegian banished from Iceland, about 982. He gave the barren land its attractive name to encourage colonists and about 986, he managed to settle 500 people there. The colony may have survived 400–500 years.

I **Iceland**, possibly visited by Irish monks, became a Viking settlement about 850–75. In 930 Icelandic settlers set up *Althing*, the world's oldest parliament. Norway imposed its rule upon Iceland in the 1200s and Denmark took it over in 1380–1944.

Icelandic sagas describe the colonization of Greenland and also tell how Bjarni Herjolfsson, a merchant blown off course from Norway to Greenland, first sighted the coast of North America about 985. The story continues with the subsequent voyages of his passenger, Leif Ericsson (Leif the Lucky) to VINLAND about 18 years later. Another story in the sagas tells how, in Greenland, Leif's sister Freydis treacherously persuaded her husband to kill some seamen from Iceland. When he would not kill their 5 wives, Freydis had them tied, then killed them herself with an axe.

Carved post from burial ship

L **Longships** had high sterns and prows decorated with figures of monstr-

The Vikings 45

Below right: The Vikings became expert shipbuilders and the most skilled seamen that Europe knew until 500 years ago. Viking *longships*, shallow and narrow in the beam, rose to a high point at prow and stern. The prow often had a dragon-like beast carved on it. Vessels with 20 oars carried about 90 men in all, and had a steering oar on the starboard side. They were easily manoeuvred in narrow creeks or shallow bays.

the complete but temporary conquest of England. In the Frankish empire they pursued more limited aims, but their conquest of Normandy was permanent. The Danes also attacked the Muslims in Spain and Morocco, and raided along the Mediterranean coasts.

Swedish Vikings traded and plundered along the inland waterways of GERMANY, but their reputation was never as bad as that of the Danes. As fierce merchant-warriors called the Varangians they settled the coastlands and lakesides of the Baltic Sea and Finland, and a group of them called the Rus daringly penetrated the rivers of the vast land which was later to be called Russia after them.

The Slav people of NOVGOROD (New City) on the Volkhov River are said to have invited the Rus leader, Rurik, to rule their city, hoping that his strong presence would bring peace and stability. Rurik founded a dynasty there in 862 which lasted over 500 years. His successor, Oleg, moved the Russian capital to Kiev about 873. Other Varangians sailed on to reach the Black Sea and the Bosphorous, raiding Constantinople in the 900s, until the Byzantine emperor bought them off, employing some to serve him as his Varangian Guard.

The Norwegians

Norwegian Vikings first seized and settled in the Hebrides, Orkney, Shetland and Faeroe islands. Their influence extended to Ireland, where they founded DUBLIN in 840 and held it until the Irish King BRIAN BORU defeated them in 1014. But the most daring Viking exploits were the Norwegian voyages to ICELAND, GREENLAND, and VINLAND (possibly modern Massachusetts). Leif Ericsson led this North American landing about 1003 and his settlement probably lasted about 12 years before being abandoned by the Norwegians. Several ICELANDIC SAGAS describe these courageous explorations into the icy north.

Before 1000, the Vikings had ceased to raid their neighbours and established stable kingdoms in Denmark, Sweden and Norway, and permanent settlements in Iceland and Greenland. Elsewhere, they integrated with the local peoples. Even the Normans evolved into the French and English, becoming staunch upholders of Roman Christianity.

ous animals. The single sail had vertical stripes of different colours, and round shields hung on the sides of the ships. They commonly had crews of 90 including 30 oarsmen.

M Myths of the Vikings are preserved in the Icelandic *Eddas*, composed 800–1300. The *Eddas* describe how, before the earth was formed, there was a northern land of clouds and darkness and a southern land of fire. Warm winds from southland melted the ice of northland, and from it stepped a human giant named Ymir. Also from melted ice, came Audumla, a cow, to provide milk for the giants. She nourished herself by licking salt from the ice, and as she licked, it melted to release another being, Buri. His son married Ymir's daughter, and their children became the gods Odin, Vili and Ve, who killed Ymir, and from his body made the earth, sea and sky. Then they made the sun, moon and stars. Odin, chief god, lived in splendour in his palace at Valhalla. His enemy was Loki, a powerful demon, who led other demons and giants in war against the gods. In the terrible destruction, gods, demons and giants died as Valhalla collapsed.

Thor, god of thunder

N Novgorod (south of modern Leningrad) probably began as a Slovane city before Rurik's time (c.860s). It remained the main centre for foreign trade after Kiev became the capital. Novgorod gained independence from Kiev in 1136, and held all northern Russia west of the Urals until 1748.

T Thor, warrior god of thunder, struck down giants and monsters by throwing his hammer, Mjolnir, at them. Thursday (Thor's day) is named after him.

V Vinland may have been the area around Cape Cod, or possibly Newfoundland. Leif Ericsson so named it because he found grapes growing there (together with self-sown wheat). A map drawn in Switzerland about 1440 has Vinland marked on it, and this may have helped later explorers of the Atlantic.

The feudal system of western Europe provided the basis of stability from which the Renaissance blossomed. Non-landowning serfs were at the base of this social pyramid, with freeholders and land-owners above them.

The Feudal Europeans

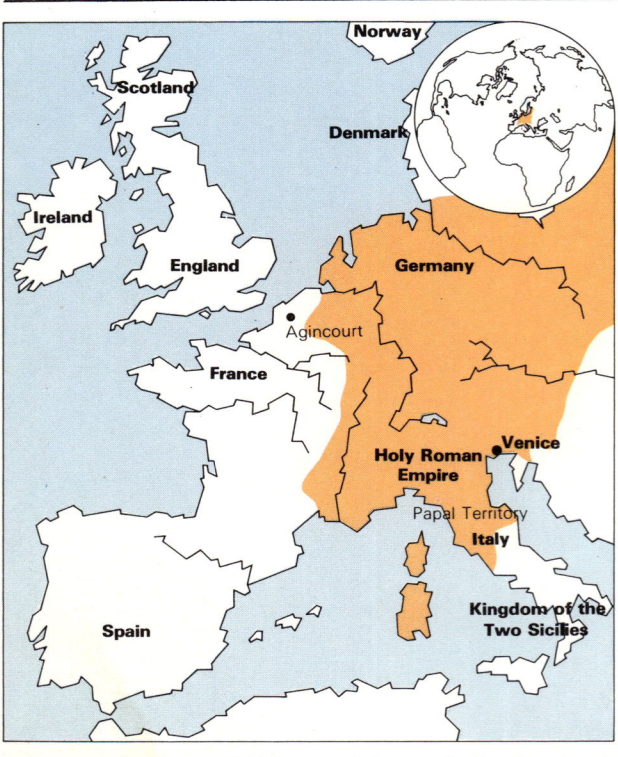

Left: Large areas of western Europe found stability in the feudal system which flourished about 1100–1300. Feudal kingdoms extended from Scandinavia to Christian Spain. The Holy Roman Empire straddled central Europe.

By about 1000, Viking raids and 'barbarian' invasions ceased in western Europe. Several kingdoms emerged, but heads of strong families sometimes held more power than the kings. These powerful lords kept private armies to fight wars both at home and abroad. Apart from the soldiers, most people worked as farmers or craftsmen in the village of their birth. They lived under the protection of the lord who owned their village, but were bound to him as SERFS. This was the basis of the feudal system, under which land was leased in exchange for services.

FEUDALISM reached its height about 1100–1300 in France, ENGLAND, GERMANY, Scandinavia, Italy and northern (Christian) Spain. Despite many shortcomings, feudalism provided the basis of stability from which the brilliant civilization of RENAISSANCE Europe later developed.

Above: Sheep became highly important as medieval Europeans exchanged their skins and furs for woollen clothes. Spain and England were noted suppliers of raw wool, but by 1400 the English processed their own wool and sold it as finished cloth.

Land tenure and class structure

In theory, all land belonged to the king, but he leased most of it to his lords. In exchange for their estates, they had to swear loyalty to him and to provide certain services, notably support in war. In England, a feudal estate constituted a manor, roughly a self-sufficient village, usually with its own castle and church. Such an estate was known as a *seigneurie* in France, a *señoria* in Spain, and a *signoria* in Italy.

Each lord possessed several estates according to his status. He had a duty to his king to protect his estates, to dispense the king's justice, and to ensure that the land was cultivated according to traditional methods. In fact, the lord seldom visited a manor, but in his absence a steward acted for him.

The lord kept much of the land on the estate as his own DESMESNE, and let out some to FREEHOLDERS in exchange for money rents. Freeholders could quit the estate at will. But most of the land was farmed by bound serfs who had to give part of their produce to the lord. They also had to provide 'week work' two or more days a week on his desmesne, and 'boon work' at harvest time. Villagers also had to pay in kind for the use of the lord's mill and oven.

Land outside the THREE FIELD SYSTEM (*see page 43*) was common. There anyone could feed cattle, poultry and sheep. Firewood could be gathered from the surrounding forest, where pigs were let loose to eat acorns. But the forests were were largely reserved as HUNTING grounds for the king and his lords and poachers, when caught, received speedy execution. Farmers slaughtered most of their animals in late autumn, and salted the meat for food throughout the winter. Only a few animals could be kept and fed for breeding in spring.

Reference

A Alchemy (an Arab word) was the non-scientific use of chemistry in an age of superstition. Alchemists sought mainly the 'philosopher's stone' which could turn cheap metal into gold; and the 'elixir of life', a drug to restore youth.

B Black Death, a virus carried by fleas that lived on rats, came from China about 1330 to reach Europe in 1348–49. Research suggests that up to 35% of Europe's people perished. In places, crops rotted unharvested in the fields through lack of labour.

C Changes in warfare brought the need for smaller, better trained professional armies. This became clear at the battle of Agincourt fought between England and France in 1415. Some 13,000 English cavalry, crossbowmen and pikemen routed 50,000 French soldiers who still used traditional tactics and techniques. Crossbows and cannon (both developed in China-Mongolia) came to dominate warfare in Europe during the 1300s. With cannon, kings could demolish castles of rebel lords and these changes made feudal armies obsolete.

Allegory of Black Death

Church, between 664 and 1521, meant in western Europe the Roman Catholic Church headed by the pope in Rome.

D Desmesne, the lord's land, often comprised half the manor. Like serfs' land, the desmesne was in the form of STRIPS scattered throughout the 3 fields.

E England was surveyed for taxation purposes by 1086 under WILLIAM THE CONQUEROR (*see page 43*). The information gathered and incorporated into the *Domesday Book*, provides a clear account of FEUDALISM in England. The king's tenants-in-chief numbered some 1,500 lords and churchmen. These subdivided their estates under 8,000 second-tenants, mainly knights.

F Feudalism derived from the medieval Latin word *feudum,* and meant a piece of land awarded in return for services.

Freeholders sometimes had to give military services

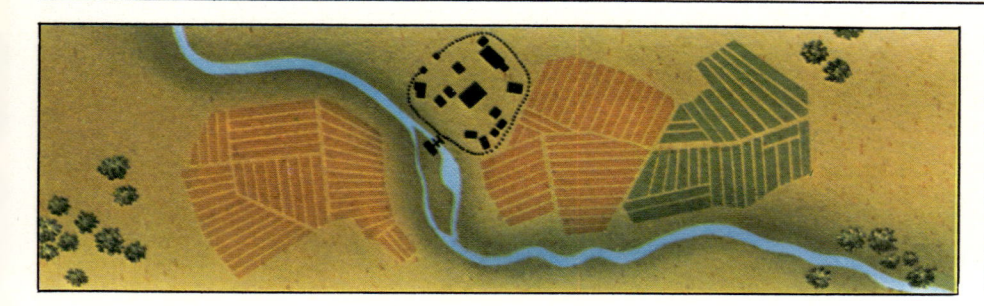

The Feudal Europeans

Left: Crop land was divided into 3 huge fields, usually rotated as wheat, barley or fallow fields on a 3-year system. Every household held a number of strips of about 1 acre scattered throughout the 3 fields. Meadow, common and heath – or wasteland – provided grazing land and firewood.

Below: Lords of the manor held their land from the king to whom they had to swear allegiance. They also had to run their estates efficiently, dispense justice, and maintain adequate military forces for defence or war. In practice, stewards usually ran the estates for the lords.

The Church

In all the feudal kingdoms, the CHURCH wielded great economic, political and psychological power. Bishops and other churchmen held land in their own right as feudal lords. Church lands tended to increase, because guilt-ridden nobles often willed land to the Church at death, hoping thereby to expiate their sins.

The popes insisted that, as God's representatives, they held power of appointment or dismissal of kings. They threatened kings and other rebels against their authority with excommunication, which would cut them off from God in this life and the next. The Church's ultimate weapon, was the authority to excommunicate a whole nation. Few kings dared to flout the power that the Church held over the minds of their subjects. On the other hand, the popes often needed the military power of strong kings to keep their own positions.

Many serious disputes occurred between Church and Crown. In 1075 Pope Gregory VII and the German emperor Henry IV began a bitter quarrel about which of them should appoint bishops. The dispute outlived them both, to be settled by their successors in 1122. Soon after, the papal lands around Rome were threatened by the massive HOLY ROMAN EMPIRE under Frederick Barbarossa (Redbeard) in the north, and the Kingdom of the Two Sicilies (ruled by Frederick's nephew) in the south. The pope broke this domination only in 1266, when he reached a deal with the French monarchy, in which a French prince annexed the Two Sicilies with papal blessing. When Pope Innocent III placed England under an interdict (1208–13), its king, John, had to submit. On the other hand, Frederick II, who between 1196 and 1229 was successively crowned ruler of Germany, Sicily, Italy, the Holy Roman Empire, and Jerusalem, flourished despite excommunication.

Below: Serfs formed the lowest rank of society after slavery died out. But changing times brought freedom and relative prosperity to some serfs by the 1300s.

Above: Freeholders formed a class between serfs and lords, able to leave the estate when they chose. Wealthier freeholders often employed serfs on their own account.

---

in exchange for their land. They also had to give boon work, but never week work. It is not fully known why a few farmers remained free

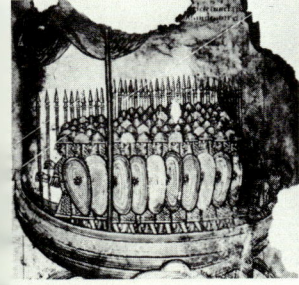

The Norman fleet lands

when most were bound in serfdom, but towards the end of feudalism, many serfs commuted (had their 'rent' changed from services to money), and so became freemen.

G **Germany** in feudal times was divided into hundreds of states, all within the Holy Roman Empire.

H **Holy Roman Empire** extended into present-day Netherlands, Denmark, Poland, Hungary, Italy and France. Otto the Great was crowned Roman emperor in 962 and the empire continued until 1806.

Hunting, mainly of deer and wild boar, was the sport of the upper class who kept vast forestlands for pleasure. Lords often drove people from their homes to turn the land back into hunting forests. The resentment of underprivileged people to such treatment has been expressed in many stories, such as the Robin Hood legends.

J **Jousting** took place at tournaments where mounted knights in armour charged each other with lances, often in front of the king. Such contests were governed by the code of chivalry.

Jousting

M **Measurements** became standardized in England by the 1300s, due to the demands of trade. They included: 1 foot (length of a shoe sole); 1 yard (width of cloth); 1 rod, pole (of an ox team); 1 furlong (furrow length); 1 acre (area of 1 strip). To end disputes, Henry I of England (reigned 1100–35) decreed that the yard should be fixed as the distance from the tip of his nose to the end of the thumb of his outstretched arm.

R **Renaissance** (rebirth of learning), the liberation

The Feudal Europeans

The feudal lord was primarily a warrior. At home, he joined alliances for or against the ruling king. Abroad, he fought alongside his king or, draped in the cross, campaigned in the CRUSADES (see page 36). He was supposed to observe the rules of chivalry – a moral and religious code that governed conduct in peace and war. Knights, originally a class of untitled warriors, supported their lords in battle and were recruited from squires, who began their military training as pages from about the age of seven. Knighthood became almost a cult, backed by its own traditions such as JOUSTING.

The break-up of the feudal system

By the 1300s, cracks appeared in the feudal system. CHANGES IN WARFARE rendered the barons' armies less efficient and when more money came into circulation, many lords found it convenient to receive money rents instead of services. Labour became scarce, and therefore expensive, and rents, traditionally fixed, could not be raised. Many lords rented out their desmesnes or turned to sheep farming.

The decline of feudalism was speeded by the BLACK DEATH, a deadly plague that killed off a large proportion of Europe's people in 1348–49. Meanwhile, new ideas from Italy shook old beliefs. In England, feudalism had largely died out by 1400 but it lasted until 1789 in France, and 1867 in Russia.

Right: Much of life in Europe of the 1400s revolved around the streets rather than behind walls. Craftsmen made their products where they sold them. Drapers, bakers and candlestick-makers plied their trades in public. Guilds imposed strict rules.

Below: One of the finest records of life in feudal England is the Bayeux tapestry, a band of linen on which were embroidered about 72 scenes representing the Norman conquest. Scenes shown include the building of earthworks for William's camp, the serving of a meal and shipbuilding. This section shows the Norman fleet setting sail.

Towns and trade

The growth of towns and TRADE also speeded the end of feudalism. Towns flourished first in Italy, then north of the Alps, located where rivers provided fresh water and transport. In northern Europe the Hanseatic League, an early 'common market' of some hundred towns linking England to Russia, dominated international trade. The economic power of wealthy merchants undermined the feudal authority of kings, lords and Church.

---

of ideas after the Dark Ages, began in Italy in the 1300s. It spread throughout western Europe in the next 200 years. It sparked off advances in religion, SCIENCE, art, exploration, technology, and economic, political and social life.

Science found little scope in feudal Europe beyond ALCHEMY. However, Roger Bacon (c.1214–92) an English friar, wrote *Opus Majus* ('Greater Work') which covered a variety of sciences. Bacon understood and believed in the value of observation and experiment, the beginnings of scientific method. Although Pope Clement IV befriended him, Bacon suffered imprisonment by the Church for the 'dangerous ideas' in his works.

Serfs comprised over 90 per cent of Europe's population. Generally, the more land a serf held the more work was required of him. Consequently, richer serfs farming perhaps 30 or more STRIPS, often employed poorer serfs to work for them. A poor serf, holding perhaps 3 to 5 strips, might work either on the richer serf's own land, or give services direct to the lord on his wealthier neighbour's behalf. This variation of serfdom speeded the end of feudalism. In England, serfs who fled from their lords to towns, became free by custom if not caught within a 'year and a day'. In England, the small number of slaves had disappeared, probably to become serfs, by 1100.

Strips varied in size but generally comprised as much land as could be ploughed in a single day. In England, a strip usually measured 1 furlong (furrow long) by 1 chain. Basic MEASUREMENTS came from farming and crafts.

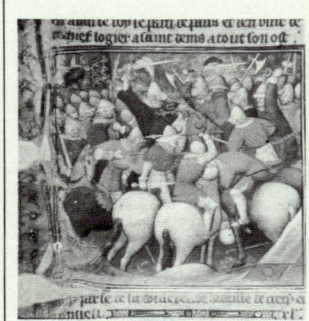

Battle of Crécy (1346)

Trade on the lords' estates barely existed beyond imports of salt, iron, and luxuries for the lord. Within towns, craftsmen produced goods on the premises where they were sold. Standards of quality, training, employment and trading, were strictly laid down by the various guilds to which merchants, masters, craftsmen and apprentices belonged.

The African cultures that developed south of the Sahara were based on trade in gold, slaves and nature crafts to the Arabs. Native arts reached a peak in the magnificent Benin bronze sculptured heads.

The Africans

While the Arabs developed their civilization in northern Africa, African cultures developed south of the Sahara, especially in GHANA, MALI and Songhai. The scanty knowledge we have about these empires comes from Arab sources, especially the writings of the Arab geographer AL-BAKRI and the great Arab traveller Ibn Batuta (1304-77). However, distinct styles of African sculpture have survived to influence modern artists and traditional African music has greatly influenced the jazz and popular music of the 20th century.

Eastern Africa

The most ancient of black African states, the kingdom of KUSH (which had once ruled Egypt) fell to King Ezana of Axum in the AD 300s. Axum (in Ethiopia) prospered by controlling much of the world's ivory supply. Ezana, persuaded by St Frumentius (a Syrian apostle to the Abyssinians) Christianized his country in 333, developed a written language, constructed palaces and churches, and spread its culture throughout Ethiopia. After northern Africa and the Red Sea coasts fell to Islam, Ethiopia remained an isolated Christian state, whose Christian culture has continued up to present times. The Europeans knew it only in legend as the 'land of PRESTER JOHN'.

Further south, along the coast north and south of ZANZIBAR, Muslim traders from the Persian Gulf and southern Arabia founded several city-states. The prosperity of these states attracted African migrants from the interior, who developed the distinct language and culture of SWAHILI. Ibn Batuta, who visited the island city-state of KILWA, wrote that it was a flourishing crossroads of trade between south-eastern Africa and countries as far east as China.

The mainstay of Kilwa's trade was gold, which came from the region of Zimbabwe. The fortified settlement of Zimbabwe, first built between 1000

Right: Except in the Arab north, Africa for a long time lay outside the mainstream of civilization. Then came African civilizations in Ghana, Mali and Songhai. Other centres of civilization included the Hausa states, Kanem-Bornu, Axum, Ethiopia and Zimbabwe.

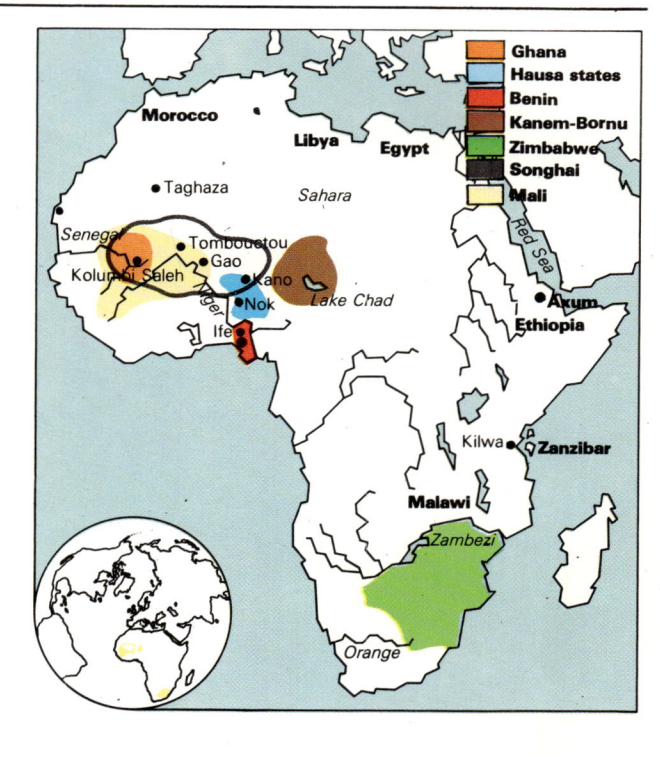

Above: This head of an *Oni* (king) of Ife, Nigeria, cast in brass in the 1200s, represents a high peak in African art. Facial features, including scarring, are finely rendered. Beads decorate the crown.

and 1400, later declined but revived under its ROZVI kings, who constructed its largest buildings in the 1500s. The settlement declined, and ended abruptly in the 1830s when Zulu warriors destroyed it.

Ancient Ghana

During the 300s, BERBERS from Libya migrated south-westwards across the Sahara and organized the MANDINGO-speaking people into the Ghanaian empire. According to al-Bakri, GHANA was the title given to the emperor, who ruled through chiefs subject to him. The Ghanaians later expelled their Berber overlords, to bring the empire under black rule by 700.

To the Arabs, Ghana was the 'LAND OF GOLD'. But the gold did not originate in Ghana. Simple

Reference

A Al-Bakri (c. 1040–94) an Arab geographer of Cordoba, compiled his *Book of Roads and Kingdoms* as a guide to Africa in the late 1000s. He collated many travellers' reports.
Ancestor figures were created in the hope that spirits of dead ancestors would come to inhabit them. If one was thought to have arrived, people treated it with great respect, for it was thought to grant favours: a good harvest, victory in war, or children to a childless woman.

B Barter was usual in African lands, where coins were rare or non-existent. In Mali, gold dust provided currency for objects of high value; cowrie shells for small change. Ibn Batuta carried beads, salt and spices to barter for his needs.
Berbers may have entered Africa from south-western Asia. They remained nomads, but became powerful in and around Morocco. The Berbers who founded ancient Ghana came from Libya and may have been of the Judaist religion.
Bronzes of Ife are really 'brasses' made from an alloy of copper and zinc.

Blue men – desert nomads

C Camels, introduced from Asia, came into widespread use for transport in Africa only during the 200s. Until then, the Sahara formed an almost impassable barrier between north and south (although oxen and horses did sometimes cross it).

G Ghana (ancient) lay north of the area where the Niger and Senegal rivers come near together in present-day Mali-Senegal. Ancient Ghana lay 600 km north-west of modern Ghana.

H Hausa states (of which Kano was the most important) were semi-independent vassal states of Kanem-Bornu. After 1513, they came under Songhai until that empire collapsed.

K Kilwa flourished as an island storehouse for ivory, copper, gold, slaves and other items. These were transported by camel caravans from as far south as MALAWI, northward to the coast. Small dhows took them to Kilwa. From Kilwa, ocean-going dhows left for southern Arabia and the

The Africans

Left: The proud figure of an African king on a horse represents one of the best pieces of bronze-working in the kingdom of Benin.

Mali

King Sundiata (1230-55) laid the basis for a new empire, Mali, which enhanced its status with the Arabs by adopting the Muslim religion. When Emperor Mansa Musa (1307-32) made the pilgrimage to Mecca, he distributed so much gold that the Cairo money market was thrown off balance. Tombouctou (Timbuktu) became a leading centre of Muslim learning, and together with Gao, a great trading centre. The Arab traveller Ibn Batuta remarked on the number of lawyers there and on the high standard of justice. He praised the schools, with their many books and classes in music and dancing, but had little respect for Mali's architecture. In the 1400s Mali underwent internal decline, speeded by attacks from the TUAREG and other southern peoples.

traders brought it from the south to the fringes of the empire to exchange it for basic necessities such as SALT from the north. The exchange took place through a strange kind of dumb barter in which the traders themselves did not speak, and usually did not even meet. Other traders then took the gold to the Ghanaian capital. This stood at the centre of trade routes along which passed ivory, gum, ostrich feathers, KOLA NUTS and slaves. Berbers kept control of the main trade routes, along which they had earlier introduced camels.

The Moroccan Almoravid movement, a religious reform movement, which had reunited all the Berber tribes in about 1042, reconquered Ghana in 1076. However, their heavy-handed intervention destroyed the trade along with the empire and the Ghanaian capital (then Kolumbi Saleh) was finally destroyed by the Mandingo king, Sundiata, in 1240.

---

east. Luxuries such as Chinese silk and porcelain came through Kilwa into eastern Africa from about 1150.

Kola nuts, a mild narcotic, were prized by the Arabs because the Koran forbade alcohol. Islam had no prohibition against kola nuts, probably because Muhammad never knew them.

Koumbi Saleh, located about 600 km west-south-west of Tombouctou, consisted of 2 towns. A large Muslim trading town with 12 mosques stood alongside the African capital.

Kush, which ruled Egypt 750–656 BC, became rich from its gold and iron. Learning from the Assyrians (who eventually chased them out of Egypt) the Kushites made iron tools and weapons.

L Land of gold was the Arab name for ancient Ghana. The king's horses wore gold-embroidered trappings; his attendants held gold-hilted swords; and courtiers had their hair plaited in gold.

Lost wax process was the African method of bronze casting. Sculptors shaped heads roughly in clay, then coated them in wax which they cooled and then carved with fine detail. Then another layer of soft clay was put over the wax, the inside being moulded exactly into the wax carving. The sculptor then poured molten metal between the 2 layers which melted the wax, and replaced its exact shape in the clay mould. After cooling, the sculptor broke away the clay to expose his work of art. Some heads are less than 2 mm thick.

Pendant cast by lost wax process

M Malawi kingdom, a loose federation based on the Malawi kings' control of local trade, reached its height in the 1600s as an ally of Portugal. The kingdom disintegrated when the Yao people of Mozambique-Tanzania seized control of the trade in slaves and ivory.

Mali was visited by Ibn Batuta, who was shocked by the freedom allowed to African women in contrast to the seclusion of Arab women. He reported that the king enforced his authority by keeping on the move with a troop of cavalry.

Mandingo-Bambara group of languages are spoken in the corner of western Africa bounded by southern Senegal-Mali and the Ivory Coast.

| # The Africans | 51

Right: The animal hunt illustrated on this rock painting from Tassili, Algeria, shows the lively movement of prehistoric art in the Sahara. Early North African paintings portrayed a wealth of animal life. Nearby, pictures have been found of war chariots, humans and animals.

Above left: Iron smelting in Africa was first practised by the people of Kush, who learned it from the Assyrian conquerors of Egypt. The picture shows an iron smelting furnace and bellows still used by some tribes in Zimbabwe.

Then a subject people of Mali, the Songhai, captured Tombouctou, Djenne and Gao and established their own empire.

Under emperors Sonni Ali (reigned 1464-92) and Askia Muhammad (reigned c.1493-1528), Songhai became the strongest African power. But Islam, which had strengthened Mali, brought the downfall of Songhai as it provoked opposition from the upholders of the old tribal religions.

The end of Songhai

Moroccan jealousy of Songhai's control of the trade routes exploded into hatred when Songhai took the TAGHAZA salt mines. In 1590-91, the Moroccan sultan, Ahmed IV (al-Mansur) sent a small army equipped with English firearms to defeat the cavalry and bowmen of Songhai. The Moroccans took Tombouctou, Djenne and Gao. They deported Songhai's learned men to Morocco and stole or destroyed their books. The Moroccan army then refused to recross the desert, and set up a weak state of their own. Mandingos and Tuaregs attacked them and the civilization of Ghana-Mali-Songhai disintegrated.

Hausa states and Kanem-Bornu

East of Songhai, several HAUSA STATES flourished, famed for their fine leatherwork, which was exported north and known as 'Morocco leather'. Around Lake Chad the Muslim state of Kanem-Bornu drew inspiration not from Morocco but from Egypt. Kanem-Bornu lacked the economic strength of Ghana, Mali and Songhai, but it grew into a formidable power under King Idris Alooma, who used Turkish firearms and military techniques. Kanem-Bornu succumbed only to European invasion in the 1880s.

The arts of western Central Africa

Nigeria has a tradition of sculpture dating back to the NOK CULTURE of 2,000 years ago. By 1200 the city of Ife (sacred to the Yoruba tribe) produced superbly sculptured heads in terracotta and BRONZE which was cast by the LOST WAX PROCESS. By 1400 African bronze heads reached new standards of excellence in the secular court art of Benin. Almost all other African art stemmed from religion, such as ANCESTOR FIGURES.

Much of the rest of African art came from the region between Nigeria and Zaire, but little survives. Objects made of perishable materials such as wood or straw rotted in the humid climate, were eaten by ants, or burned in war. Muslims and Christians destroyed the works of art they found, damning them as false idols.

Although the number of languages spoken by the peoples of Africa was about 2,000, their music had a common pattern, bound up with drums and dancing. Essentially spontaneous, it nevertheless kept within traditional patterns of melody and rhythm. One purpose of the drum dance (especially in religious ceremonies) was to work the dancers up to a frenzy of religious zeal, so the drumming was hectic and insistent.

Religion, and mythology

African religion, like African art, had a common basis. At one level was the belief in a supreme god; at another level there was a belief in many gods and the power of the spirits of ancestors. Men had to live at peace with these powers, therefore the supposed intermediary between man and the gods was a specialist in magic known as a witch-doctor. Age-old folk myths gave explanations for every aspect of daily experience. Africans recited these tales from one generation to the next, for (outside Ethiopia) they had no written languages.

A Songhai tale told of a chief who went fishing at night and found a small sheep in the middle of the river. As he recited magic spells in fright, the sheep turned into a baby. The chief shouted for help, knowing he had seen a ZIN (water spirit). When the villagers found the chief he was dead, for the sight of a Zin meant death for mortals.

N **Nok culture.** Several finely-sculptured terracotta heads, dating from over 2,000 years ago have been found at Nok in Nigeria. Nok people probably used iron from about 400 BC.

P **Prester John,** a legendary Christian priest-king, was supposed to have lived in the 1100s. Marco POLO (see page 28) and other travellers claimed that he once ruled over a large kingdom in central Asia. Later, the Portuguese claimed that he ruled in Ethiopia. Prester John was said to have been descended from a Persian Magi.

Nok head

R **Rozvi,** a clan of the Shona tribe, constructed several stone buildings in the Zimbabwe area. Local tribes imitated these in wood, wattle and mud in villages in the Zambezi-Orange rivers region.

S **Salt,** vital to life, could not be found where it was most necessary — the humid forest land. Consequently, the forest peoples collected gold to trade for it. **Swahili** means coastal people in Arabic. Swahili people are of mixed descent, mainly Afro-Arab. Swahili is also the name of their African language with Arab admixture. It is now the chief commercial language of eastern Africa.

T **Taghaza,** the salt city in northern Mali, had houses built from blocks of salt roofed with camel skins. Ibn Batuta visited it in 1352. Antonio Malfante, an Italian bank agent, reported seeing salt houses 95 years later. He visited Mali to search for the source of African gold which was then pouring into Europe.

Tuareg, a Berber people, now live mainly in the Air Mountains region of the Niger Republic. The Tuareg dialect has a writing system partly derived from ancient Berber.

Z **Zanzibar** flourished from early times as an island trading centre between Africa and Asia.

Zin, supposed water spirits, may have derived from Arab *djinn* (fire spirits). One of these was the djinn or *genie* of Aladdin's lamp.

The uniqueness of Japanese arts and crafts stems from the fact that they evolved in relative isolation from the Asian mainland. Origami, Kabuki theatre and flower arranging are just some of the new art forms that flourished.

The Japanese

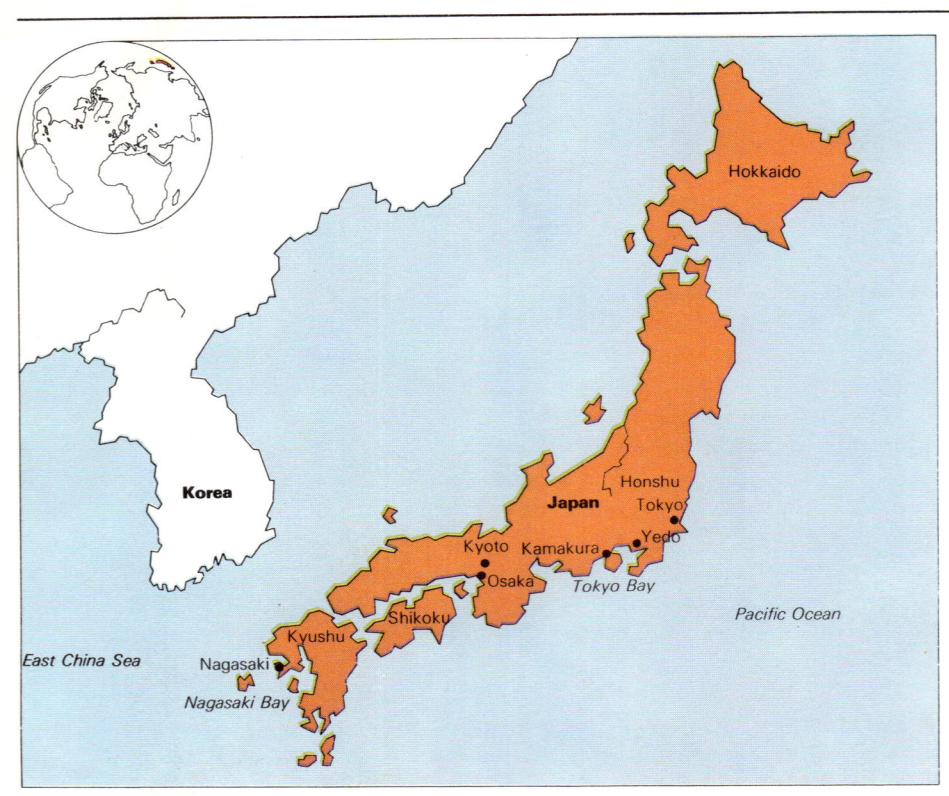

Cut off by 200 kilometres of sea from the Asian mainland, Japan developed in isolation. Earthquakes, volcanic eruptions, storms and winds lashed the rocky, infertile Japanese islands, giving rise to the belief in an infinite number of *kami* nature spirits. These were thought to control every aspect of life within the religion of SHINTO. Into Japan's closed society of the mid-500s came Chinese priests bringing BUDDHISM, along with China's art and written language. From this clash of cultures emerged a new civilization, which incorporated amongst other things, several unique arts.

Above: Japan developed both because of its isolation and its nearness to China, from which it borrowed heavily.

Above: Expressive masks cover the faces of all-male actors in Japan's highly stylized Nō plays.

Emperors, feudal lords, and shoguns

In 794, Emperor Kammu established his capital at Kyoto. From there, his descendants reigned as gods for over 1,000 years, although they had little authority. As in medieval Europe, the real power lay with feudal families, or *clans*, who fought unceasing civil wars. Eventually, about 858, the FUJIWARA CLAN gained power and reduced the emperors to puppet status.

The Fujiwara ruled for 300 years, but then split into two factions, one of which called in the Taira clan to fight its battles; the other faction called in the Minamoto. Both clans had ambitions to oust the Fujiwara, and the Taira finally succeeded about 1160. Once in power, they constructed harbours, dredged shipping channels, developed trade with China, and generally improved the economy. But the Minamoto overthrew the Taira in 1185.

The Minamoto set up their *bafuku* (military government) at Kamakura (near Tokyo Bay), and in 1192 persuaded the emperor to give Minamoto Yoritomo the title of SHOGUN. MINAMOTO SHOGUNS ruled from Kamakura until 1333 when Ashikaga Takauji became first of a line of Ashikaga shoguns who ruled from Kyoto.

The Ashikaga shogunate

The Ashikaga shogunate was a period of turmoil during which the power of the shoguns often sank as low as that of the emperors. Local lords increased their power but many warriors lost their status to become peasants. Meanwhile some poor people pushed their way up into a new aristocracy.

The upheaval led to certain improvements. Cultural activities flourished, encouraged by the shoguns and ZEN Buddhist monks, and metal-working, weaving, papermaking and other industries expanded. Many small market places grew into bustling towns and the new city of Osaka grew to rival Kyoto. As a result TRADE WITH CHINA boomed.

Reference

B **Buddhism** and Chinese ideas met determined resistance in Japan although they were eventually accepted. Prince Shotoku, regent 593–621 and 'founder of Japanese civilization', actively encouraged Chinese culture.
Bunraku, the Japanese form of puppet theatre, reached its height under the romantic dramatist Chikamatsu Monzaemon in the 1600s.

D **Dutch** traders were the only 'red-haired barbarians' (the Japanese name for Europeans) allowed to remain in Japan after 1636. Those who came to trade were penned in on a small man-made island in Nagasaki Bay. Chinese merchants could also trade with Japan, under strict control.

F **Fujiwara clan** gained power by constantly marrying Fujiwara girls to reigning emperors. They then reduced the emperors' activities to SHINTO duties, making them little more than puppet emperors.

K **Kabuki** is a lively form of drama still popular today that developed from dancing. It contains elements of NŌ and BUNRAKU, but is less stylized than these.

Golden Pavilion, Kyoto

M **Minamoto shoguns**, in power 1185–1219, mostly lacked the forcefulness of Minamoto Yoritomo (1147–99). From his death, his widow's family, the Hojo, totally dominated the shogunate.
Mongol attacks on Japan started in 1274. The Mongol navy first attacked the islands, where the garrisons fought to the death. Later they landed in Kyushu despite fierce resistance, and when a severe storm threatened the Mongols' ships, the Mongols fought their way into Kyushu again in 1281, but a typhoon destroyed their fleet. Shinto and Buddhist priests took credit for the *Kamikase*, or Divine Wind, that saved the country.

N **Nō plays** combine dancing, chanting and music into a slow-moving, simple drama with a simple plot.

O **'Opening-up'** of Japan began in 1853

The Japanese

Left: Fujin, god of the winds, carries his bag of winds slung across his shoulders. Japan's Shinto-Buddhist religion includes the belief in an infinite number of *kami* (spirits), which may vary from a volcano to a tree or even the concept of happiness.

Below: The tea ceremony, performed as a ritual, is one of several uniquely-Japanese arts that combine national traditions with deep symbolic meanings.

Japan and the outer world

KUBLAI KHAN (*see page 27*) attacked Japan in 1274 and again in 1281, but with help from the weather, the Japanese beat off both MONGOL ATTACKS. The next foreigners to land in Japan, the Portuguese, brought two disrupting innovations: firearms, about 1542, and the Roman Catholic religion. Despite Buddhist opposition, the Roman Catholics claimed 300,000 converts within two generations.

In the late 1500s, a humbly-born general, Toyotomi Hideyoshi (1536–98), seized power from the crumbling Ashikaga shogunate. He invaded Korea in 1592 and 1597, but the Chinese forced him to withdraw. His successor, Ieyasu (1542–1616) founder of the Tokugawa shogunate (1603–1867) crushed Christianity in Japan and sealed its island borders. For over 200 years the threat of execution hung over Japanese trying to leave Japan, or foreigners trying to enter.

The Japanese also built ships and put to sea in expeditions financed by feudal lords and merchants. By 1400, Japan dominated the East China Sea, which was rife with Japanese pirates.

The unique art of Japan

By 1600, Japanese artists had mastered Chinese techniques in sculpture, ceramics, woodworking, jewellery, lacquer, bronze, architecture, painting and calligraphy. They produced their own, essentially Japanese styles in an amazing variety of media and fashion, swords and sword furniture, miniature gardens and ORIGAMI became new art forms. Ladies of culture were marked by their skill in delicate flower arranging and by their peaceful and ritualistic tea ceremonies.

Literature paralleled the development of these visual arts. One of the world's greatest novels, The TALE OF GENJI, was written by a Japanese lady of court nearly 1,000 years ago. NŌ PLAYS, BUNRAKU and KABUKI developed as unique forms of drama, unrivalled in the western world.

---

when Commodore Perry of the US navy anchored his fleet off Japan. He demanded stores and the opportunity to open up diplomatic relations. The talks were unsuccessful but Perry returned in 1854 to impose trading relations upon Japan. Having allowed Western civilization in, the Japanese borrowed heavily from it and in 50 years they had defeated China and Russia in war and founded an empire.

Origami comes from 2 Japanese words, *ori* (fold) and *kami* (paper). Paper folding was taught from generation to generation in old Japan and Japanese books on origami appeared from the early 1700s.

S **Shinto** religion has its basis in nature and ancestor worship. Shinto priests and Buddhist monks initially clashed in Japan but eventually became integrated. Buddhists tended to be more politically involved than Shintoists, who were generally dedicated to religious affairs.

Shogun, an old title for army commanders, had fallen into disuse before the MINAMOTO SHOGUNS took it. It meant 'a great general who subdued barbarians'.

Bunraku puppets

T **Tale of Genji,** written by Lady Murasaki about 1008, gives an insight into the sophisticated court life of the time. Japanese courtiers wrote in classical Chinese when their European counterparts could seldom write their own names.

Trade with China boomed in Ashikaga times (1338–1568) as silks, porcelain, paintings, books and manuscripts made their way into Japan. Through China too, came goods from southeast Asia and India. Japan's exports of timber, mercury, mother-of-pearl, sulphur and gold, were supplemented by new manufactures such as swords, and decorated fans and screens. The Japanese had no money, so they imported Chinese copper cash as currency.

Z **Zen,** a Buddhist creed for scholars, warriors and aristocrats, involved meditation and a rigid self-discipline. The aim was enlightenment, or an understanding of the inner-self. It influenced art, the tea ceremony, flower arrangement, and rock and sand gardens.

Genghiz Khan and his savage nomadic Mongol hordes built up the largest empire the world has ever known. But they also enabled eastern and western cultures to meet. The magnificent Taj Mahal in India was a development of Mughal art.

The Mongols

Mongol peoples drained the energies of the Chinese from the beginnings of their history by constant invasions. Tribes later called 'Huns' speeded the end of the Roman empire, and Turkish tribes seized the leadership of Islam from the Arabs. By about 1300 the MONGOLS had burst across Asia into Europe to build the largest empire that the world has ever known.

Although these savage conquerors spread terror across two continents, they also brought benefits. Through them, Chinese culture spread to Persia and beyond, and East and West came into full contact for the first time.

The nomadic way of life
Having been pushed north of the Great Wall of China by the Chin emperors (221–206 BC), the Mongols inhabited the inhospitable Gobi desert, and land westwards to central Asia. Mounted on small HORSES, they wandered this arid area in search of pasture for their sheep, cattle and goats. These provided them with their basic necessities: MILK, cheese, cheese curds, meat, furs and skins.

Mongol populations moved like large armies, with teams of oxen dragging wooden waggons that held their vast tents, or GER. In the drier regions, the Mongols harnessed Bactrian (two-humped) camels to pull their high-wheeled carts. Constant movement, meant hard work – loading pack animals, guiding wagons, hunting and defending the camps. Both men and women wore a long, sack-like garment fastened at the neck, over trousers, and in freezing weather they donned fur coats and caps.

The Mongols were SHAMANISTS, whose witch doctors claimed to mediate between humans and the world of spirits. Tengri, their supreme god, ruled over this spirit world, assisted by lesser deities. Fire was sacred as a purifying agent, and execution came to those who polluted running water.

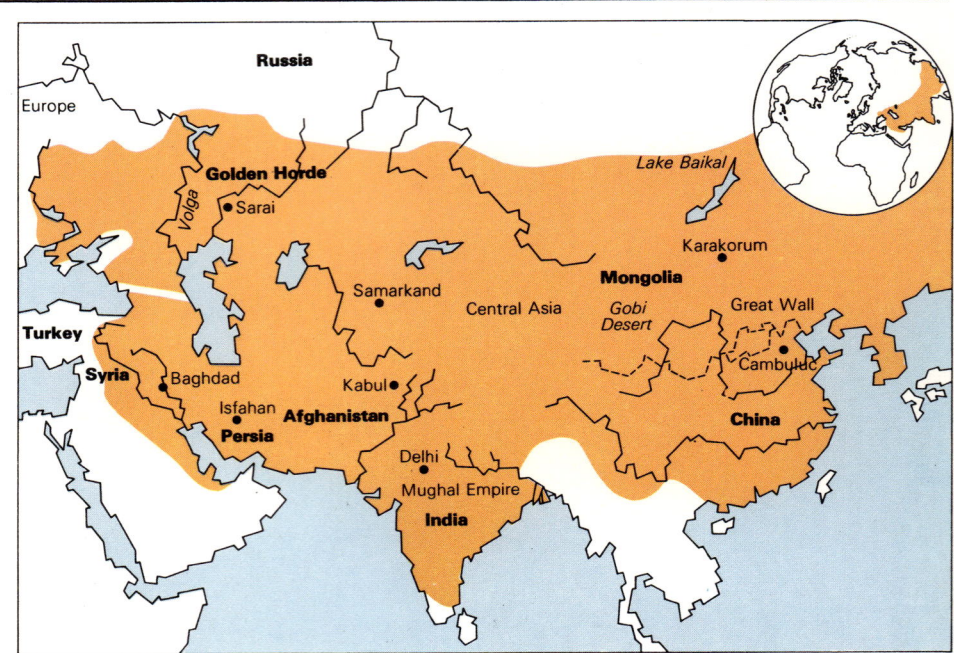

Above: Mongol conquests spread like wildfire across Eurasia in the 1200s from China into central Europe, dwarfing earlier empires.

Reference

B Baber (1483–1530), prince of Ferghana in 1495, fought the Uzbeks to take Kabul in 1504. He took Delhi in 1526 and set up the Mughal empire that controlled most of India until the 1700s.
Batu (c. 1200s), led the 'Golden Horde'. This Mongol group, with its capital at Sarai on the Volga River, was so named because of the magnificence of Batu's camp. Later, TIMUR conquered its territory.
Bows and arrows. Lightweight arrows had a range of up to 200 metres and heavy arrows were used for shorter ranges. Some Mongol soldiers carried swords or sabres with shields, while heavy cavalry used lances, and wore head armour. Mongol armies took over the military technology of conquered countries. From Chinese firearms they developed cannon.

G Ger, Mongol round tents, were constructed of felt stretched over wooden frames, set in circles with the doorways facing south. The interior of a ger had 2 compartments. Women lived and cooked in the eastern compartment; men lived and entertained in the western one. The chief male of the ger had his couch by the central hearth, directly under the smoke outlet. Several idols made of felt watched over the ger's inmates. Khans and chiefs had similar ger but greater in size. They could be collapsed or transported erect in giant ox carts. The word 'yurt', often confused with 'ger', meant the homeland (Mongolia).

H Horses, kept in herds of up to 10,000, were carefully tended. Up to 20 spare mounts followed each rider.
Hulagu (1217–65), sent to quell a revolt in Persia, wiped out the ASSASSINS (see page 34) in 1256. He sacked Baghdad in 1258, took

Mongol encampment, Afghanistan

The Mongols

Genghiz Khan and his successors

In 1206, the Mongols united under Temujin, a military leader of genius, better known as GENGHIZ KHAN (1162–1227). He set up his capital at KARAKORUM. In 1212, filled with the idea of a heavenly mission to rule the world, Genghiz Khan began the piecemeal conquest of China. His armies swept westwards through central Asia, Persia and southern Russia, to threaten the Byzantine empire. Before his death in 1227, Genghiz nominated his shrewd, genial but drunken son Ogodei (1185–1241) to succeed him. After Ogodei's death, BATU (a grandson of Genghiz) looted and laid waste to eastern Europe, and another grandson HULAGU destroyed Baghdad in 1258, savagely killing a million people. Meanwhile, KUBLAI (a third grandson), completed the conquest of China. Ruling from Cambuluc (Peking), he became nominally Great Khan of all the Mongol empire by 1260. But Kublai had little real power outside China. Local khans warred against one another and the empire soon disintegrated.

Right: Marco Polo, his father and uncle, are presented to Kublai Khan, conqueror of China. The European artist has 'Italianized' the 4 Mongols standing at the rear, not knowing what they looked like.

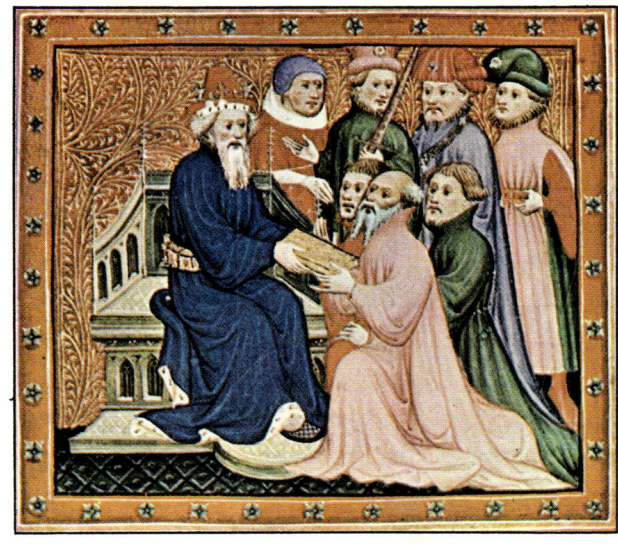

Left: The giant Mongol bow hangs from one side of this horseman's belt, his quiver of arrows at the other. In the background, his comrades complete the erection of a *ger*, or portable tent. The Mongols lived, moved and went to war as one single community. Although usually outnumbered by their victims, they almost always won through superior organization.

The Timurids and the Mughals

Just as the Mongols were leaving China, the Mongol Khan TIMUR THE LAME (Tamerlane), took southern Russia in 1369 and set up his capital at Samarkand. Persia, Afghanistan, Mesopotamia, Syria and eastern Turkey soon fell to him. Timur, a brutal conqueror who built pyramids of human skulls, was nevertheless a devout, educated Muslim who encouraged art and science.

When Timur sacked Delhi (in 1398), he destroyed the Sultanate and over a century of instability followed. Then, in 1526, BABER, a descendant of Timur, established the Mughal empire from Delhi. This empire finally fell to the British in the 1700s. By then, the Mongols had become an obscure people confined to the bleak, Buddhist land of Mongolia.

Damascus and Aleppo in 1260, but was held by the Egyptian MAMLUKES (*see page 37*) in Syria. Hulagu withdrew eastwards, became a Muslim, and founded the Il-khan dynasty in Persia. It disintegrated in 1335.

Isfahan is half the world', wrote travellers of the 1600s. Shah Abbas (1557–c.1628) of the Safavid dynasty drove the Turkic tribes out of Persia but lavished Timurid styles of architecture on Isfahan. Timurid paintings inspired Persian miniatures.

Karakorum, Genghiz Khan's military capital, was also a nomadic trading centre. Ogodei built a palace there which was visited by foreign ambassadors.

Kublai (1216–94), emperor of China 1279–94, was known for his tolerance of other religions and patronage of the arts. He became well-known to Europeans from the book by Marco POLO (*see page 28*).

Milk products drunk by the Mongols included *kumiss*, fermented mare's milk, which was alcoholic.

Mongols probably originated south-east of Lake Baikal. They formed the nucleus of a larger group of people, including Turks and Tartars, collectively known as Mongols. On their marches, Mongols added many peoples to their army, including Chinese, Afghans, Arabs, other Muslims and Europeans. The descendants of these multi-lingual armies are now integrated into the populations of at least 20 countries.

Mughal art developed from the fusion of Timurid-Persian and native Indian styles. Its greatest achievements were the magnificent Taj Mahal and detailed Mughal miniature paintings.

Shamanists believed that the visible world was dominated by invisible forces or spirits. Shamans (medicine men or witch doctors) were supposed to control these spirits in the interests of their followers. Shamans were also considered to be the wise men of the tribe, acting as priests, doctors, teachers, judges and war leaders.

Timur the Lame (1336–1405) claimed descent from Genghiz Khan and seized the old territories of HULAGU. His tomb at Samarkand is like a tall GER.

Genghiz Khan in battle

Much of the history of the Maya and their neighbours remains something of a mystery. Their society was built on slavery and a popular revolt may well have brought about their downfall.

The Central Americans

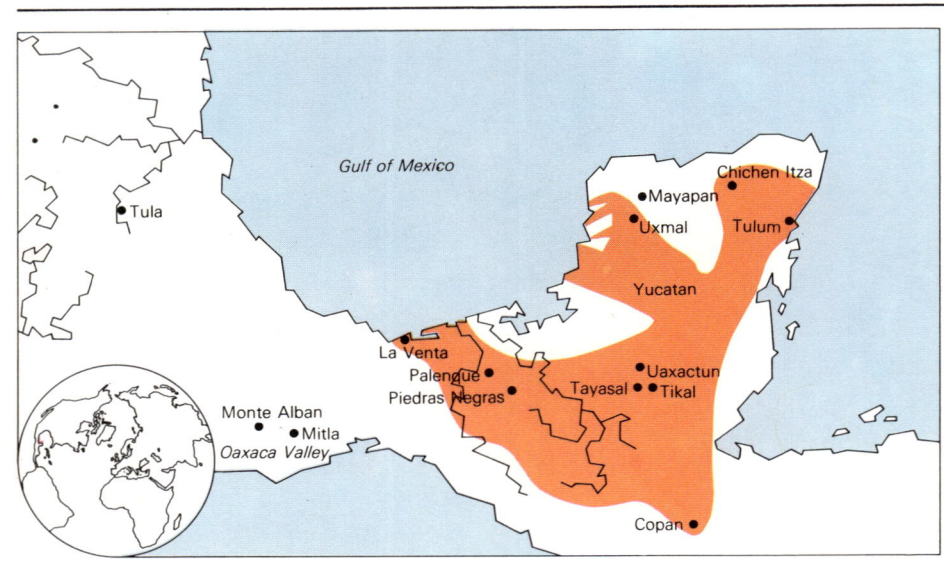

Above: The Mayan civilization stretched from Chichen Itza in the north to Copan in the south.

The humid plain of Yucatan juts riverless into the Gulf of Mexico. It is monotonously flat, with thin soil barely sufficient to support the thorny scrub found in the north. This gives way to tropical forest in the central area, which peters out as it approaches the rocky mountains to the south. This unfavoured spot and its surrounding area became the heartland of the first-known American civilizations. The Olmecs came first, a people known for carving huge STONE HEADS. A later people, the Maya, achieved spectacular success in ASTRONOMY and arithmetic and developed hieroglyphic writing. Yet they had no iron, ploughs or wheels, and no cattle, sheep, pigs, goats or horses.

Early civilizations

The Olmec civilization sprang up about 1200 BC, west of Yucatan. There, north-flowing rivers deposited silt to make the coastal plain more fertile. At the island site of La Venta, the Olmecs constructed a pyramid temple characteristic of those in later cities of ancient Central America.

Right: The ball game played by several Central American peoples took place in long, rectangular courts. Players from opposing teams tried to knock a 15 cm diameter ball through a stone ring fixed high above them.

Reference

A Astronomy was studied by Maya priests. They had no glass or optical instruments, but recorded changes in the position of heavenly bodies by sighting them through crossed sticks in relation to fixed features on the horizon.

B Ball game (*pot-a-tok*), was played in most Maya cities, in long rectangular enclosed courts. The aim was to knock a rubber ball about 15 cm in diameter through a stone ring set high in the centre of the court. Players wore protective hip pads, belts and gloves, and could hit the ball only with their fists, elbows or buttocks. Maya pictures suggest that the game was taken very seriously. In one, a player can be seen standing over the decapitated body of another. Scholar's suggest that they represent the victorious and defeated captains.

Bar and dot system of arithmetic was jealously guarded by Maya priests, although merchants used it to some extent. Like Gupta dynasty India, the Maya used the zero. They developed not a decimal, but a

Stone ring in ball court

vigesimal (based on 20s) system. The bar and dot system had only 3 signs: a dot and bar represented 1 and 5 and the zero symbol was a shell. Like the Indians, the Maya used their skill in arithmetic for religious purposes, referring to supposed dates millions of years earlier.

C Cacao beans were the money of Maya society and an able-bodied slave could be bought for 100 beans. Unwary people sometimes accepted counterfeit beans, the insides of which contained only sand.

Calendars became an obsession among Maya priests, who had several which they used in combination to find auspicious days. The *Haab* year had 18 months, each of 20 days and 5 'unlucky' days. The *Tzolkin*, a sacred calendar, had 20 periods of only 13 days. The *Long Count* calendar, using the *Haab* year, dated from a year corresponding to 3113 BC. Maya priests knew of 2 other calendars, one geared to the moon, the other to Venus.

Clothes for male peasants

The Central Americans

The other main traces of Olmec civilization, the huge basalt heads, stood two to three metres high and weighed up to 40 tonnes. As the stones for these heads had to be transported from a spot over 130 kilometres inland, transportation posed problems for the central Americans. Although the Olmecs mounted their toy clay figures on wheels, neither they nor any other American peoples put the wheel to practical use. The Olmecs carved miniature figures in jade as part of their jaguar-cult religion. Yet they remained a STONE AGE people, using only flint or OBSIDIAN tools. The Olmecs also invented systems of writing and arithmetic.

About 200 kilometres south-west of the Olmec settlements, around the Oaxaca Valley, the Zapotecs built a civilization that reached its peak about 300–900. The Zapotecs believed that their ancestors (whom they worshipped) sprang from trees, rocks and jaguars. About 600 BC, the Zapotecs levelled a hill site overlooking Oaxaca Valley to construct the pyramidal buildings of their capital, Monte Alban, where many art treasures have been found in tombs.

Above: Masks modelled on skulls form a common theme of Mayan art. The mask shown, made from some 200 pieces of jade, had shells for eyes. It was found in the sarcophagus of a secret tomb at Palenque.

The Zapotecs reconstructed the city several times, and built a religious centre at Mitla, where they worshipped Cosijo, the rain god, and other deities. A collective priesthood ran the Zapotec kingdom, constantly organizing sport and warfare. The Zapotecs used the BAR AND DOT SYSTEM of Olmec arithmetic and this and other features of Olmec-Zapotec culture were taken over by the Maya. The beginnings of Maya civilization in Yucatan go back to before 1000 BC, but the greatest Maya period coincides with that of the Zapotecs (300–900). Much of the history of the Maya and their neighbours remains unravelled, and several mysteries remain to be solved.

The Maya and their cities

The Maya were a short, dark people. Men stood on average about 1·5 metres high and women about 1·4 metres. In the tropical heat, they wore few clothes, but two Maya customs particularly affected their appearance. In their civilization an elongated head was the sign of beauty, so they strapped boards to the head of each infant, thus flattening the front part to produce a receding forehead. Mothers even dangled beads before the eyes of their babies to make them grow up with a squint, a feature that was also considered beautiful.

Between 300 and 850, the Maya built many cities, including Copán, Palenque, Piedras Negras, Tikal, Tulum and Uaxactún. Temples, shrines, palaces, baths and other buildings were constructed as pyramids with steep staircases leading to the tops. Scholars once believed that only priests and officials lived in these cities. They thought that other people lived in clearings made in the jungle by cutting and burning the trees, and moved every two or three years as their crops exhausted the soil. However, excavations at Tikal suggest that an area of about 130 kilometres around the central square was crowded with family compounds. Each compound had a plot of farmland around its buildings, where crop rotation was probably practised. Good ROADS connected Maya cities.

The ruling hierarchy included feudal lords who, as in Europe, received produce and services from the peasants. SLAVES usually received tolerable treatment, but they could be sacrificed to the gods at any time, or, after a knock on the head, be entombed with their dead masters.

---

comprised little more than loincloths, sometimes with moccasins of deerskin. Women wore a *kub*, a piece of decorated cloth with holes cut for the arms and head, over a light petticoat. Both sexes kept a square of heavier cloth used alternatively as coat, blanket, or draught-excluding curtain.

D **Dancers** impersonated deities and wearing claws and masks they danced to the music of trumpets, rattles and drums. This supposedly ensured good harvests, successful hunting or other boons from the gods, to whom flowers and maize were offered.

H **Human sacrifices** included boys aged 6–12; slaves; and high-ranking prisoners-of-war. Sometimes priests skinned the corpses so that they could then dance in the skins and occasionally they ate the flesh of their victims.

Hunters used bows and arrows introduced from Mexico in the 900s. The Maya set traps and snares and shot birds with clay pellets from blowpipes. The prey were retrieved by hunting dogs.

I **Itza** rulers either went as hostages to Mayapan,

Toltec stone figures

once defeated, or trekked to Lake Peten Itza. There they founded Tayasal, the last independent Maya state.

M **Maize** was shelled and cooked by Maya women, then ground into flour. From maize, women made *tortillas*, flat, unsweetened pancakes. Tortillas were rolled into pipes and served as spoons with which to scoop up other food before they too were eaten. Maize was also made into dumplings or gruel. It was the staple food, and so a god in its own right.

O **Obsidian**, a glassy volcanic rock, was made into tools. Priests used obsidian knives to cut out the hearts of HUMAN SACRIFICES.

P **Pictographic language** of the Maya was written into colour books made from the treated bark of wild fig trees. Spanish priests destroyed all the books or *codices* that they found. But 3 somehow made their way to museums in Dresden, Madrid and Paris and Russian scientists deciphered parts of them with the aid of a computer.

58 The Central Americans

Left: Chichen Itza is a ghost city with well-preserved architecture of the pyramidal type typical of ancient America. It has the largest ball court in Central America. In the foreground stands the sacred jaguar, set by a temple dedicated to the jaguar cult.

The staple diet of the Maya included MAIZE, beans, root crops, sweet potatoes and pumpkins and several kinds of fruits and spices were grown, including melons and chillies. Doves, ducks, curassows (turkey-like birds), and a breed of hairless dogs were fattened for eating, and fish, snails, and the larvae of mud-wasps were added to the diet. Deer, wild pigs, armadillos and tapirs were hunted.

CACAO BEANS, roasted, ground, and mixed with maize flour, provided a chocolate beverage while stingless bees produced the honey to make a fermented drink. Other stimulants included cactus juice, tobacco, and the hallucinatory drug mescalin, from the peote plant. The resin of copal trees provided incense for the temples; rubber trees gave the material for making rubber balls; and from chicle trees came chewing gum. Cacao beans were prized for being more than a food: they passed as currency in a society otherwise without money.

Gods, priests and scientists

The Maya heaven had 13 layers above earth, and the Maya hell nine layers below. Beneath the supreme but remote god, Hunab Ku, lesser deities included QUETZACOATL (Feathered Serpent), a god shared with other peoples. At frequent religious ceremonies, DANCERS impersonated deities, while priests freely sacrificed birds and animals, and occasionally humans. Worshippers often drew blood to please the gods.

Below: This ceramic vessel was made by a Toltec craftsman who worked without the potter's wheel. Toltecs, from the Mexican highlands, were probably the warriors who reoccupied Chichen Itza about 930.

The partly-hereditary priesthood had many functions. Priests kept the CALENDARS and so decided when planting and harvesting should begin, buildings be constructed or WARS begin. Much concerned with time, the Maya erected stone slabs to record the end of each *katum*, or 20-year period. As keepers of horoscopes, the priests took to astrology, which led them on to astronomy and they were able to calculate accurately the solar year and predict eclipses. The priests, who kept arithmetical records, using the bar and dot system of the Zapotecs, dominated Maya art and the PICTOGRAPHIC LANGUAGE.

Even *pot-a-tok*, a strange Maya BALL GAME, had religious associations. Spectators sat in tiers watching players attempt the near-impossible task of knocking a ball through a high stone ring. Betting was heavy on popular players.

The ghost cities

For some unknown reason the Maya abandoned their cities by about 850, leaving the jungle to reclaim them. Some scholars think that a popular revolution occurred in which the peasants killed their priests and rulers. As a result people moved from one area to another, and the 'old empire' ended. The ITZA, a people who, according to their own records, had abandoned the city of Chichen Itza centuries earlier, returned to it about 930. With them came a warrior people, probably TOLTECS, whose leader was named Feathered Serpent.

The old empire people hated the newcomers, who brought with them new styles of art with stiffly-carved figures of warriors. The invaders founded new cities, including Uxmal and Mayapan and their new empire flourished for over a century, before disintegrating into civil war. Peace came in 1194, after the Itza suffered defeat by the warriors of Mayapan. The tyrannical rulers of this city dominated Maya territory until 1441, then their subjects rebelled, killed their rulers and sacked the city.

Yucatan then split into many tiny city-states fighting ceaseless civil wars. Decline was speeded by a devastating hurricane in 1464, and an unknown epidemic in 1480. In 1511 the first Spanish invaders arrived, bringing with them smallpox and ultimately, the end of Maya independence.

Q Quetzacoatl (Feathered Serpent), a god shared between Toltecs and other peoples, took many forms. He supposedly discovered art, science, MAIZE and the CALENDAR. He is identified with the cult hero, Kukulkan.

R Roads, built by peasants to a width of 4.4 metres, linked Maya cities. Tough, roughly-hewn stones formed a foundation, surfaced with gravel or limestone chippings and cities had raised, paved causeways. Only the Incas built better roads in the Americas.

S Slaves among the Maya came from 4 main classes. They included children sold by impoverished parents; orphans; convicts enslaved as a punishment; and low-ranking prisoners-of-war.
Stone age culture in central America was general, except that the Maya made splendid figures in gold and copper. Nothing has been found to indicate that they mixed tin with copper to make bronze.
Stone heads of the Olmecs were probably floated down river on huge rafts. They probably represent Olmec rulers.

T Toltecs, a warlike people, built an empire in the Mexican highlands about 750. Their leader, Topiltzin, who founded Tula in the 900s, added the name QUETZACOATL (Feathered Serpent) to his own name. In 1224, the Toltecs fled Tula after it was sacked. The warriors who reoccupied Chichen Itza about 930 were probably Toltecs.

W Wars were fought usually in the dry season, when agricultural tasks had finished. All men bore arms and women accompanied them to war to prepare meals. Battles ended at nightfall, when food was ready. Maya soldiers sought to capture rather than kill the enemy. Wars ended when one of the leaders was taken prisoner. He and his officers then became sacrifices. Soldiers fought with shields, clubs, daggers, lances, tridents and (from the 900s) bows and arrows. They wore padded 'armour' of cotton soaked in brine.

Olmec stone head

The Aztec god, Huitzilopochtli, needed constant nourishment in the form of human blood, in return for which he promised the tribe domination over the neighbours. The Spanish conquistadores *put an end to their domination.*

The Aztecs

While the Olmecs, Zapotecs and Maya built up civilizations in and west of Yucatan, other, inter-related cultures developed farther west. One small tribe, the Mexica (or AZTECS), grew out of obscurity to found a great empire. But the WAY OF LIFE of this talented people was tainted by their obsession with BLOOD SACRIFICE.

Teotihuácan: Zapotecs and Mixtecs

About 100 BC, an unknown people began to build Teotihuácan (Place of the Gods) – the biggest city of central America housing about 200,000 people. For some mysterious reason the city was abandoned about 750. This coincided with the decline of the Zapotecs of the Oaxaca Valley whose culture came under the domination of the Mixtecs, craftsmen who produced fine works of art in stone, metal, wood, bone and pottery. After subduing the Zapotecs in a series of long wars, the Mixtecs took over Monte Alban and Mitla. The Zapotec-Mixtec wars halted in the late 1400s when the two enemies combined to fight a new warrior people from the north: the Aztecs.

The wanderings of the Aztecs

According to their legends, the Aztecs took their name from Aztlán (White Land), the supposed place of their origin. About 1111, they began a long migration in search of a home. For a while they settled near the old ruined Toltec capital of Tula. There, they learned simple agricultural techniques, irrigating farmland and building CHINAMPAS ('floating gardens'). They entrusted their fate to their god, Huitzilopochtli (Humming-bird). This god, according to Aztec priests, needed constant nourishment in the form of human blood. In return, the priests said, Huitzilopochtli promised the Aztecs domination over their neighbours, but he ordered them to leave Tula and resume their wanderings.

Just before 1300, the Aztecs reached the city of Chapultepec in the Valley of Mexico, the centre of the Toltec civilization. After the collapse of the Toltecs and the suicide of their last king, many people had migrated to the valley. The Aztecs, being the last to arrive, met opposition. Those Aztecs who survived the ensuing massacre, threw themselves on the mercy of the city of Culhuacan, which had already sacrificed the Aztec leader to its own god. Surprisingly, the Culhua granted the Aztecs some nearby land.

Although it was only a snake-infested rocky wasteland, the Aztecs prospered. They intermarried with the higher-cultured Culhua, and proudly called themselves 'Culhua-Mexica people'. However, as allies, the Aztecs proved so fierce that, in about 1345, the Culhua tried to exterminate them. Culhua soldiers forced the Aztecs back to the edge of a swampy lagoon. Desperately, the Aztecs made rafts from javelins and spears padded with coarse grass. On these, they floated out to the safety of a small, reed-choked island in the lagoon. The Aztecs had reached their final home.

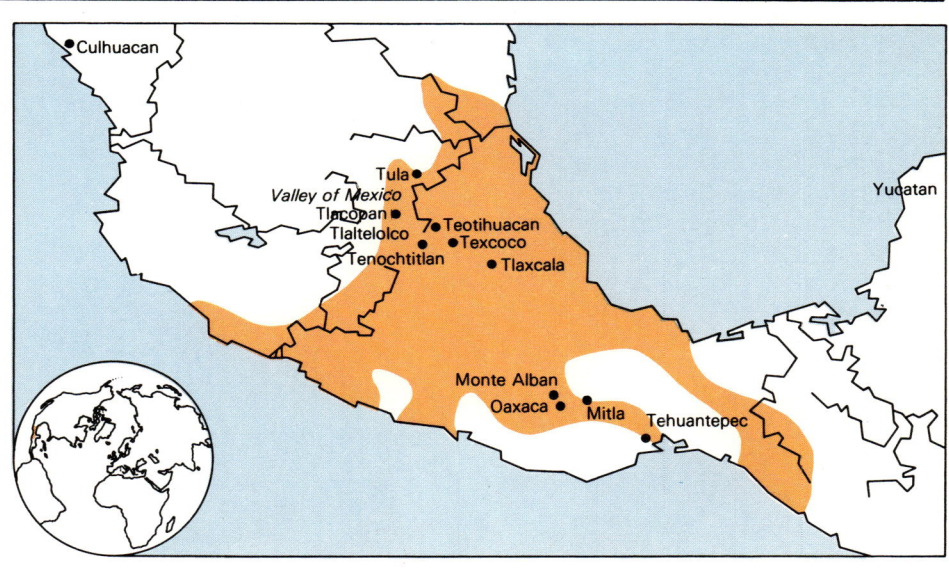

Above: The civilization of the Aztecs began with a small settlement at Tenochtitlan. This city grew to became the capital of a vast empire under Montezuma.

Above: A human skull was used to shape this Aztec mask – a mosaic of turquoise, sea-shell and lignum. It may represent Tezcatlipoca (Smoking Mirror) the great sky god.

Reference

A **Artefacts** included the 'Aztec Calendar', really a sun stone dedicated to Tonatiuh, the sun god. His face adorns the centre of the stone, and claws are carved gripping human heads. The stone symbolizes the eternal struggle between Quetzacoatl and Tezcatlipoca (Smoking Mirror) — evil god of the night sky. These and other symbols on the stone represent the Aztec idea of the nature of the universe.

Aztecs, according to tradition, changed their name to *Mexica* or Mexicans on the orders of Huitzilopochtli, who then gave them a net, bow and arrows. After this, the Aztecs shot arrows expertly. *Mexica* came from the word *meztli* (moon) in the Nahuatl language spoken by the later Aztecs.

B **Blood sacrifice** claimed over 20,000 victims a year and horrified the Spaniards. The Aztecs were equally shocked that the Spaniards burned people alive. At least sacrifice brought a quick death because priests cut out the heart with obsidian knives within seconds.

Stone calendar

C **Chinampas**, misnamed 'floating gardens' were tiny island 'farms' built in shallow fresh water. In Tenochtitlan, agricultural land being scarce, the Aztecs cultivated the shallow lagoon. They made platforms from layers of mud and water plants walled in by basketwork. Intersected by canals, these formed excellent land for crops.

Codices, a term denoting manuscripts in book form, also describes the picture books of ancient Mexico painted on tree bark, deerskin, or 'paper' made from agave leaves. Aztec 'books' were either rolled up into scrolls or folded like modern maps.

Cortés, Hernando (1485-1547) sailed to Hispaniola in 1504 and Cuba in 1511. When he landed in Yucatan in 1519, Cortés recruited a shipwrecked Spanish sailor who spoke the Maya language. He also received the gift of an enslaved princess, Malinche, who knew the speech of the Maya (Putum) and the Aztecs (Nahuatl). On the march towards Tenochtitlan, Cortés recruited the Tlaxcalans as

The Aztecs

The Aztec struggle for supremacy

Settled on the island, the Aztecs first built a simple shrine to Huitzilopochtli. Around it grew the city that became TENOCHTITLAN. Thirteen years later, the Aztecs built a second city, TLATELOLCO, on a nearby island. The peoples of Tenochtitlan were warlike; those of Tlatelolco were merchants and traders. Through trade, the Aztecs prospered, but three strong powers surrounded Tenochtitlan, ready to cut off its supplies. Unable to survive alone, the Aztecs had to choose an overlord. They therefore offered allegiance to the TEPANECS, who claimed to be the heirs of the unknown builders of Teotihuácan.

Through three generations the Aztec-Tepanec relationship changed. The Aztecs progressed from a state of humiliating subservience to junior partnership, and eventually to rivalry. To rid themselves of Tepanec domination, the Aztecs entered into a triple alliance with the anti-Tepanec state of Texcoco and with Tlacopan (a breakaway Tepanec city). After defeating the Tepanecs in 1428, the triple alliance continued, dominated by the Aztecs. Gradually, some five million people came under the rule of the Aztec empire in a 1500-kilometres-long territory from north of Tenochtitlan to Guatemala. Under MONTEZUMA (Moctezuma) II, ninth king to rule from Tenochtitlan, the promises of a great empire said to have been made by Huitzilopochtli, came to fruition.

Above: A macabre artefact from the civilization of the Mixtecs is this ornamental knife made of chalcedony. It was used to cut out the hearts of human sacrifices. Skilled in anatomy, priests killed their victims within seconds.

The Aztec way of life

Tenochtitlan, joined to Tlatelolco and several smaller islands, grew to become a city of some 165,000 people. Causeways with movable drawbridges linked it to the mainland in the north, west and south, and canals gave access to all parts of the city. Fresh water from hillside springs supplied the city through an aqueduct. Among the city's most impressive buildings was the magnificent pyramid raised to Huitzilopochtli. Lesser DEITIES had their own temples and special sacrifices.

Left: The caricature of human sacrifice by Aztec priests was painted from memory by a man who, in his youth, had been a subject of the Aztec emperor. Temple orderlies drag away the body of a victim from the foot of the temple steps. In front of the temple, a priest has just cut out the heart of a second victim, which he holds up. A second priest has held the victim's legs as he stretches backwards over a stone block awaiting the knife. The blood-smothered temple contained racks for the dead men's skulls. Priests ate the flesh of their victims at certain ceremonies.

---

allies. In Tenochtitlan, he took MONTEZUMA hostage and tried to govern through him. In 1520, during Cortés's absence from the city, his deputy unwisely began a fight with the Aztecs. After Cortés's return, the Aztecs besieged the Spaniards. During a battle, Montezuma stood on a battlement to try to bring peace. The Aztecs (who had already rejected him) threw stones, one of which hit his head and killed him. (Other versions of his death exist.) The Spaniards retreated to Tlaxcala, but recaptured Tenochtitlan in 1521. They annexed all Mexico, which they called 'New Spain'.

D Deities below Huitzilopochtli included Tlaloc, the rain god; his sister, the water goddess; Tlazolteotl, goddess of love; and Coatlicue, earth goddess and mother of Huitzilopochtli. The Aztecs also worshipped Quetzacoatl, universal god of central America. These deities had their own temples and human sacrifices. By each temple stood a huge rack holding thousands of skulls. All deities had their special sacrifices and ceremonies.

Tlaloc, god of rain

E Evil omens troubled MONTEZUMA before the arrival of the Spaniards. One was the accidental burning of a temple. Another was a large bird with a mirror in its head, said to have been brought to Montezuma by priests; when he looked into it he saw the stars in daylight. Looking again, the king saw many warriors who seemed to be part men, part 'deer'. (The Aztecs had never seen horses.)

M Montezuma II (reigned 1502-20), was the Aztec emperor at the time of the Spanish invasion under CORTÉS. He was regarded as a demi-god but was finally stoned to death by his own people who regarded him as a traitor.

O Oaxaca in the late 1400s was a mainly Zapotec city under Mixtec rule. Although Monte Alban had been abandoned for centuries, the Mixtecs used it for burials, and fine goldwork has been found in its tombs. Some Zapotecs had moved southwards to Tehuantepec to retain their independence.

Aztec craftsmen dyed cloth expertly, made distinctive pottery of quartz and clay, and produced fine jewellery and ARTEFACTS in stone, jade, silver and gold. The Aztecs recorded important events in 'books' of 'paper' made from agave leaves. They used a pictographic script similar to that of the Maya. In Montezuma II's time, the Aztecs produced the CODICES which recorded the organization of the empire and the payment of tribute.

All goods that did not travel by water were carried by men. Agricultural techniques remained primitive, digging sticks being the main implements. Tribute arriving in Tenochtitlan from subject tribes included rubber, feathers, cacao, and precious metals and stones. People also paid taxes to the government in the form of food, clothing, skins, silver, gold and feathers. Aztec warriors had similar equipment to Maya soldiers, except that they wielded swords made of obsidian.

The end and the beginning of time

Like the Maya, the Aztecs combined their solar and sacred calendars to find auspicious days. Time, they believed, was granted by the gods in 52 year cycles. At sunset on the final day of the cycle, people climbed to the summit of Huixachtecatl (Hill of the Star), an extinct volcano. From here they anxiously scanned the sky for a certain star.

At the exact moment when the time cycle ended, a priest kindled a fire in the open breast of a newly-killed human victim. This macabre ceremony would help to ensure that the world would go on. As the vital star passed the centre of the sky, the whole Aztec nation sent up a shout of joy, for the gods had allotted a new cycle of time for the world.

The end of the Aztecs

From the time of his accession in 1502, Montezuma fought wars of annexation around OAXACA. Nearer home, a war begun against Tlaxcala and its allies in 1504, brought no quick victory. As the conflict dragged on over 13 years, the king grew more and more haggard and depressed, and vindictive towards his priests and astrologers. Aztec accounts say that many EVIL OMENS came to trouble him. Then, in 1519, came reports of 'mountains moving in the sea'. These were Spanish ships heading for Yucatan, where the Spaniards were welcomed as RETURNING GODS.

After a brief clash, the Tlaxcalans and Spaniards joined forces. This pact sealed the Aztecs' doom. Two years later, Hernando CORTÉS, leading 1,000 Spaniards armed with guns, horses and iron weapons, captured Tenochtitlan for the second and final time, and put an end to the Aztec civilization.

Above: Aztec *tonalamatl* were the reference books of the priests. They were made from paper made from the beaten bark of the wild fig tree. Paper-makers cut them into long strips which they coated to take paint, then folded them like modern maps. Either one or both of the open pages related to affairs of a particular week. Artists drew the controlling deity of the week extra large, and other figures represented subordinate deities or symbolized objects of worship. In the remaining space, ruled-off squares contained the 13 day-names and numbers, and the deities in their various forms.

Left: This jade mosaic jewel set in gold is one of many fine examples of Mixtec artistry.

R **Returning gods.** According to legend, Quetzacoatl vanished with the fall of the Toltec empire, and his return was expected from the sea to the east. MONTEZUMA, thinking CORTÉS was the returning god, sent envoys with presents to meet him in the old Olmec territory. They came back with Spanish presents for Montezuma, who had them buried in Quetzacoatl's temple in Tula with appropriate sacrifices.

T **Tenochtitlan** or present-day Mexico City, was named after Tenoch, chief priest-ruler of the Aztecs when they reached their final home. He died about 20 years after the founding of the city. This would be 1325 if the traditional Aztec date is taken. But many scholars think 1345 is more likely. Estimates of the city's peak population vary between 60,000 and a million.

Tepanecs settled west of the lagoon in which Tenochtitlan was later founded, and built Azcapotzalco (Place of the Ant Heaps) as their capital. It is now a suburb of Mexico City. The Tepanecs became in turn the oppressors, tutors, partners, rivals and subjects of the AZTECS. When the Aztecs first arrived, they and the Tepanecs formed the 2 great civilizations seeking to fill the gap made by the Toltecs' collapse.

Tlatelolco developed as a city-state in its own right, set up its own dynasty and even fought a brief war against Tenochtitlan in 1473. Although the war quickly ended, Tlatelolco lost independence.

W **Way of life.** Many people in the Aztec empire lived in remote villages, in adobe huts with thatched roofs. Men worked in the fields, while women cooked food such as tortillas and spun and wove cloth. Men wore capes and loincloths; women wore sleeveless blouses and calf-length skirts. Colourful decorations on clothes showed the wearer's position in society. Lesser chiefs wore white; priests wore black.

All that remains of Chinampas, the 'floating gardens'

The Inca emperors were supposedly descendants of the sun. They organized Inca society broadly as a welfare state at the expense of individual liberty. However, they pioneered 'pensions' for the old and work for the disabled.

The Incas

Left: The empire of the Incas extended 4,000 km north to south, straddling the Andes through what is now Ecuador, Peru, Bolivia, Chile and north-western Argentina.

Above: The quipu, an ingenious system of recording numbers by means of coloured knotted cords, could also store coded messages. An hereditary class of quipu keepers kept and interpreted the quipus.

Civilizations emerged along the Andes Mountains and the western seaboard of South America in about 1000 BC. Several cultures, centred on present-day Peru, rose and fell over a period of 2,500 years. Although the peoples of Peru and Yucatan (4,000 kilometres to the north-west) shared the same ORIGINS, no evidence has come to light to suggest that they were in contact. They had, however, several features in common: both civilizations constructed pyramidal buildings and had broadly similar art forms, and in religion, both had BLOOD SACRIFICE and a JAGUAR CULT. The Inca tribe set up their capital at Cuzco (300 kilometres north-west of the sacred LAKE TITICACA) in about 1200, and had incorporated most neighbouring peoples into their EMPIRE by 1476. INCA EMPERORS, supposed descendants of the sun, organized society broadly as a socialist state; used bronze tools and weapons; devised a unique system of counting; kept good ROADS; and introduced the potato to the rest of the world. However, they did not use the wheel, money or a written language.

Early civilizations

In South, as in Central, America, the ruins of several mysterious ancient settlements still stand. The oldest-known, Chavín de Huántar, lies high in an Andean valley over 1,000 kilometres north-west of Lake Titicaca. It dates from about 700-200 BC. Chavín's large, well-built stone temples have colourful sculptures of complex symbolism. Chavín art comprises ceramic ware, textiles and goldwork. Its styles influenced the arts throughout the surrounding region.

On the southern shore of Lake Titicaca, on a plateau 4,000 metres above sea level, stood TIAHUANACO, believed to have been the religious and political capital of the AYMARA INDIANS before AD 500.

While Tiahuanaco still flourished, the Chimú culture developed around the Moche River. Its capital, Chan Chan (1,300 kilometres north-west of Lake Titicaca) covered 15 square kilometres. At its centre stood ten walled buildings, which were probably palaces. Chan Chan's tombs once contained gold and silver artefacts, jewellery, textiles and ceramic ware and scales were found for weighing precious metals and stones. Because no system of writing existed, nothing records the history of these cities beyond their material remains. However, from their artefacts, it appears that they heavily influenced the civilization built up by the Incas.

Reference

A Adobe, mud mixed with straw, was sun-dried to make bricks for houses.
Aymara Indians occupied the Lake Titicaca area and probably built TIAHUANACO. Though conquered by the Incas, their descendants still live there and speak their own language.

B Blood sacrifices among the Incas consisted mainly of llamas, guinea-pigs or birds. However, up to 200 children might be sacrificed to mark the coronation of a new emperor, or to persuade the gods to intercede in defeat, plague or famine. Victims included prisoners-of-war and children collected as 'taxes'.

C Clothes of alpaca or llama wool were at a later stage supplemented by cotton. Men wore sleeveless tunics over breechcloths (a type of loincloth) and turbans and women wore long dresses with sashes. Both sexes had long cloaks and leather sandals.
Criminals who killed while robbing were put to torture before execution. Manslaughter was sometimes punished by exile to the emperor's coca plantations. Sabotage, bribery and corruption often carried the death penalty.
Crops included maize, root crops, peppers, peanuts, avocadoes and pineapples. Tomatoes were introduced into South America from Central America and potatoes originally grew around the Peru area, before spreading throughout the world.

E Ear ornaments were a sign of the wearer's nobility. A noble's son had his ears pierced to show that he had become a warrior.
Empire of the Incas extended 4,000 kilometres north to south through modern Ecuador, Peru, Bolivia, Chile, and the north-western tip of Argentina.
Farming implements of the Incas surpassed those of Central America. The *taclla*, (foot plough), a 2-metres long pole with bronze or hardwood point, had a footrest and handle. Bronze-bladed hoes and stone clod-breakers were used.

H Hunting in the Inca empire was a privilege reserved mainly for the royal

Bolivian women weaving

The Incas

Left: Machu Picchu, lost city of the Incas found only in 1911, is perched high in the Andes near Cuzco. Surprisingly, the Spaniards never knew of its existence.

The Inca empire

Inca, the name for the emperor, the empire and the tribe, derived from the name of the ruling family. Inca legends do not go back beyond 1200, when the first Inca emperor is said to have begun his reign.

Inca history begins with the ninth emperor, Pachacutec Inca Yupanqui (reigned 1438-71) who probably built the city of Cuzco. He and his son Tupac Inca (reigned 1471-93) achieved a series of lightning conquests. Under father and son the empire expanded to cover nearly 100,000 square kilometres with perhaps eight million inhabitants, but it lasted only two generations (1476-1534).

The very existence of the Inca empire marked a triumph over geography. Most of its forts, towns and cities including Cuzco, MACHU PICCHU and Ollontaytambo stood far up in isolated mountain valleys in the Andes. Despite the absence of wheeled vehicles, good roads connected these mountain settlements with outposts of the empire, linking the hot, rainless deserts of the north to the tropical wet coastlands of the south.

The welfare state

The Inca empire was a despotism, with an absolute ruler, supported by a hereditary aristocracy, where all people had their place; the family, nobles, workers and slaves. Nevertheless the well-being of each social order was taken into account. Censuses were taken and local government was geared to units of ten. Each ten heads of family had a leader, and each 40,000 families a governor. In conquered territories, local officials were kept on to implement the Inca system. They imposed their own language, Quechua, upon the whole empire; bureaucracy thrived, and government inspectors enforced social and moral codes diligently. One of their many duties was to call from house to house checking that women were good housewives and mothers.

Begging was unknown and unnecessary in this welfare state. Officials provided 'pensions' for OLD PEOPLE in the form of food and other necessities. They also allotted suitable work to disabled people and regulated their lives: blind persons could marry only other blind persons, and dwarfs had to marry dwarfs. However, strict laws governed peoples lives. Able-bodied boys

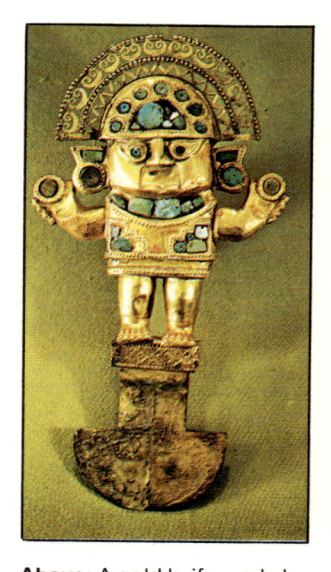

Above: A gold knife made by a Chimu craftsman was intended for use in religious ceremonies rather than in sacrifices. The Chimu god figured on the handle was absorbed into the Incas' pantheon.

---

household, although it was permitted to others at certain times. Slings and clubs provided the main hunting weapons.

I Inca emperors supposedly date from 1200. Seven of the 13 reigned before 1400. Little is known about them except that they fought constant war against neighbouring states.
Inca temples served as living quarters for priests and attendants. The Temple of the Sun in Cuzco was plated with gold. Ceremonies often took place in the central square of Cuzco. The chief priest of the Temple of the Sun (probably a close relative of the Inca) headed the priesthood of the empire.

J Jaguar cult was widespread from about 850 BC and dominated the Chavín culture. The jaguar was probably the chief deity. People believed that certain men could turn themselves into jaguars at night.

L Lake Titicaca, sacred to the Andean people, is the subject of many legends. One tells that in pre-Inca times the Sun failed to rise. After much praying, the Sun rose from an island in the

Inca baths

lake and at the same time, a white father figure appeared from the south working miracles like a god. People called him *Ticci Viracocha* or *Tuapaca*. Some of the teachings of his cult matched those of Jesus. This may account for the speedy Christianization of the Incas.

M Machu Picchu, most visited of the Inca cities, lies 80 km north-west of Cuzco, perched high on a rock between two mountain peaks. A 'lost city' until 1911, Machu Picchu was found largely intact. It may have belonged to the early Incas.
Mummies. Coastal people buried their dead in deep sandy graves after first wrapping them in cloth, then the skin of a sea lion or a woollen blanket. The bodies were buried in a sitting position, heads propped on knees. In the dry sand they became dessicated (dried out) and mummified.

O Old people, kept by the state, were expected to make themselves generally useful around the house. Officials found disabled people suitable jobs. For ex-

64 The Incas

and girls of marriageable age lined up in front of the governor for the boys to choose wives, and the governor settled pairing disputes on the spot. Torture or death came to those who left one district for another without permission and CRIMINALS received just but severe sentences.

Agriculture
Unlike the Central Americans, the Incas had two useful animals. Alpacas provided wool for CLOTHES and llamas served as light pack animals. Although llamas did not pull ploughs, the Incas had much better FARMING IMPLEMENTS than the Central Americans. Highland PLOUGHING began in August, and farmers had to till land belonging to the government and temples first, then their own. The chief CROPS included potatoes and maize from which they made *chicha* (a rough alcohol). They also chewed the dried leaves of the coca plant as a narcotic. HUNTING was a privilege reserved for the nobility although fish were caught along the coastlands and in lakes.

Medicine, science and technology
Like the Maya, the Incas practised the strange custom of flattening babies' heads by pressing them between boards. Surgeon-priests practised TREPANNING (cutting, drilling or scraping out parts of the skull).

The Incas used pebbles in a tray as a kind of abacus and weighed with scales and stone weights, but their main device for recording numbers was the QUIPU. They measured the time of day by the position of the sun, and probably had three ten-day weeks in a month. Extra days were added occasionally.

Early Peruvians were well advanced in metallurgy. Inca bronzesmiths produced a variety of articles, ranging from axes to tweezers and ceremonial objects.

Architecture, art and religion
The Incas and their predecessors built with ADOBE and stone. Their stone WALLS interlocked exactly and needed no mortar. The Incas did not use the arch, but the roofs of earth tombs around the Moche River have a form of arching. Houses had wall vents for ventilation, but no chimneys; smoke escaped through the doorways.

INCA TEMPLES housed priests and cult objects rather than worshippers. Religious practices included offerings to Viracocha (the supreme god) and other deities; fasting, consulting oracles; 'reading' the organs of animals; omens; and blood sacrifice. At religious ceremonies people danced frenziedly and became drunk from *chicha*. At death, they looked forward to either a luxurious heaven or a comfortless hell. Myths and legends surrounding the many deities often incorporated fabulous animals. Inca religion also included nature worship, stone worship, cult heroes, the concept of a great flood, and belief in the creation of successive races of men by the deities.

The end of the Incas
When Tupac Inca died in about 1487, Huayna Capac succeeded him. At his death in 1525, the empire was divided between his two sons, Huascar (c.1495-1533) and Atahualpa (c.1500-33). By 1532 Atahualpa had imprisoned Huascar in a bid to win the whole empire. At this stage came invasion by some 177 Spaniards equipped with horses and firearms. Led by Francisco Pizarro (c.1470-1541), the Spaniards ambushed Atahualpa and held him hostage. Although the Incas paid an enormous ransom for Atahualpa, the Spaniards broke faith and killed him. In spite of civil war among the Incas, organized popular uprisings delayed the complete Spanish conquest until 1539. In time, Peru became part of the empire of the western Europeans.

Above: Boats made from reeds, called 'little sea horses' by their makers, have been used for perhaps 2,000 years on Lake Titicaca.

Above: Naturalistic scenes painted in bright colours make many Inca pots particularly distinctive.

---

ample, blind persons cleaned the seeds from cotton.

Origins. The ancestors of the peoples of ancient America almost certainly came from Asia. Probably they walked over from Russia to Alaska before the 90 km Bering Strait formed. Mongoloid features can be seen in present-day descendants of the migrants.

P Ploughing involved the men moving ahead in line while their womenfolk followed, breaking the clods of soil with hoes.

Q Quipu was a device consisting of several knotted cords attached to a main cord. The colour, length and thickness of the knots indicated different numerical values. Quipus could also record coded messages. A hereditary caste of quipu keepers kept accounts and decoded messages. They guarded their secrets jealously.

R Roads. Although they inherited good coastal and mountain roads from earlier peoples, the Incas did not use the wheel. They maintained and improved the roads so that armies, human porters and pack llamas could move about speedily. Messengers, running in relays, provided a communications system with relays every 2-3 km.

T Tiahuanaco predated AD 500. Its great gate of the sun cut from one stone block and adorned with carvings, once formed part of a ceremonial enclosure. This, and other stones weighing up to 100 tonnes, had to be transported several kilometres.

Trepanning (removal of pieces of the skull) was practised by Inca surgeon-priests. More than half of their 'patients' survived. Possibly they treated soldiers clubbed on the head, to relieve pressure on the brain. Occasionally, gold plate was used to cover the cavity where the bone had been removed.

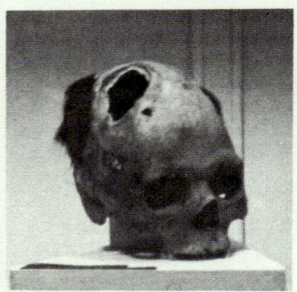

W Walls of the Andean buildings had their stones interlocking exactly. They withstood earthquakes – unlike modern buildings.

Skull showing trepanning, Peru

Index

Page numbers in **bold** type refer to the reference sections.
Page numbers in *italics* refer to illustrations.

A
Aachen, **40**, *40*
Abbasids, **33**, 35–6
Abd al-Rahman, **33**, 38
Abu Bakr, 33–4
Acropolis, **3**, *6*
Administration,
 Frankish, **40**
Adobe, **62**
Aeschylus, **3**
Africa(ns), 49–51
 Ancestor figures, **49**
 Arabs and, 50–1
 Art(s), 49–50, 51
 Iron smelting, 50–1
 Music, 51
 Mythology, 51
 Trade, **49**, 50, 51
Agincourt, *46*
Agriculture,
 English, **43**
 Feudal European, **46**, 46–7, **48**
 Inca, **62**, 64, **64**
Ahmed IV, 51
Ajanta caves, **30**, *30*
Al-Bakri, 49
Alchemy, **46**
Alcohol, Muslims and, 33
Alexander the Great, **14**, *14*, 15, *15–6*
 Death, **14**
 Ideals, **14**
 Legend, *15*
Alexandria, **14**, *15*, 17
 Scholars at, 17
Alfred the Great, **42**, *42*, 43
Alhambra Palace, *33*, **36**, 38
Ali, Caliph, **33**, 34
Al-Kindi, **33**
Al-Masudi, 37
Almoravids, 50
Americans, Central (Maya/Olmec/Zapotec), 56–8
 Art, *57*
 Astronomy, **56**
 Clothes, **56**
 Map, *56*
 Mathematics, **56**
 Money (Cacao beans), **56**
 Pictographic language, *57*
 Roads, *58*
 Sport, **56**, 56–7
 Wars, *58*
Amphorae, Greek, **3**, *3*, *7*
Ancestor figures, African, **49**
Angkor, **30**, *30–1*
 Khmers and, 32
Angles, 17
Anglo-Saxon Chronical, **42**
Anglo-Saxons, *see* English
Animals,
 Paintings, *51*
 Roman, *17*
Antioch, 24
Apollo, **3**, *7*
Aqueduct, Roman, *19*
Aquitani, **12**
Arabian Nights, **33**
 Harun al-Rashid and, 36
Arabs, **31**, 33–9
 Africans and, 50–1
 Architecture, **34**, *34*, 36–7
 Art(s), **34**, *34–5*
 Astronomy, 36
 Christians and, **37**
 Geography, 37, **38**
 Islam and, **33**
 Law, **37**, 38
 Map, *33*
 Science, 36
 Slaves, 39
 Society, **35**
 Spain and, 38
 Trade, 36, 38
 Travellers, **33**
Archimedes, **6**
Architecture,
 Franks, **40**
 Greek, **3**, *3–5*, 5–6
 Inca, **62–3**, *63*
 Indian, 30–1
 Mongol, **54**, 54–5
 Muslim, **34**, *34*, 36–7
 Pagoda, 52
 Roman, *18–9*, 19, 23
Arians, **3**
Aristophanes, **3**
Aristotle, **4**, *4*, **8**
Army, Roman, 20–1
Art(s),
 African, 49–50, 51
 Arab, 34–5
 Aztec, 59
 Celtic, **12**
 Chinese, 26–7, 29
 Etruscan, **10**, 11, *11*
 Franks, **40**, *40*
 Inca, 63–4
 Indian, 30–1
 Japanese, 53
 La Tène, **12**

B
Baber, **54**
Bacchus, *23*
Bacon, Roger, **48**
Baghdad, 33–4, **35**, *35*, 36
Ball game, Mayan, **56**, *56–7*
Barbarians, **17**
Barley, **17**
Barter, **49**
Bathing, ritual, 32
Baths,
 Inca, *63*
 Roman, *19*
Batu, **54**
Bayeux tapestry, *48*
Beaker people, **12**
Bede, Venerable, **43**, *43*
Belgae, **12**
Benin bronze, *50*
Beowulf, **42**
Berbers, **35**, 39, **49**
Bireme,
 Greek, *9*
Black Death, **46**, *46*
Blue men, 49
Books, Aztec paper, *61*
Borobudur, **30**
Brian Boru, **44**
Buddha, *32*
Buddhism, **28**, **52**
 Zen, **53**
Bukhara, **33**
Bunraku, **52**, *53*
Burgundians, **17**
Byzantines, 24–5
 Architecture, **25**
 Map, *24*
 Missionaries, **24**
Byzantium, **3**, **4**, *24*

C
Caedmon, **42**
Caesar, Julius, **17**, 18
Cairo, **33**
 Market, **33**
 Mosque, *34*
Calendar,
 Aztec, **59**, *59*, 61
 Maya, **56**
Caligula, *18*
Camels, **49**, *49*
Canute, King, 43
Capet, Hugh, **40**, 41
Capital, Byzantine, 24
Carolingians, 41
Carthage,
 Galley, *9*
 Hannibal and, **20**, *20*
 Punic Wars and, **22**
Celsus, 21
Celts, **10**, 12–13
 Art, **12**
 Christians and, **42**, 43
 Deities, **12**, *12*
 Druids, **12**, *12*
 Map, *12*
 Sacrifice, **12**, *13*
 Society, **12**, *13*
 Tribes, **12**
Central Americans, *see* Americans, Central
Ceramics, Chinese, **27**, **28**, **29**
Chaeronea, **14**, *14*
Chalcedon, Council of, 24
Chan Chan, **62**, *62*
Chang-an, **26**
Charlemagne, **24**, **41**, *41*
 Empire, *24*
Chavín de Huantar, **62**, *62*
Cheng Ho, Admiral, **26**
Chichen Itza, **56**, 58
Chinampas, **59**, *61*
Chinese, Later, 26–9
 Arts, 26–7, 29
 Drama, **28**
 Gunpowder, **26**
 Money, **26**, **28**
 Porcelain, **27**, **28**, **29**
 Printing and books, **28**, **29**
 Town planning, 27
 Trade, **26**, 27–8
 See also individual dynasties
Chivalry, **47**, *48*
Cholas, **30**
Christianity, 21, 24
 Islam and, **35**, **37**
 Celtic, **42**, 43
Chu Wen, **26**
Chu Yuan-chang, **26**
Church,
 Feudal European, **46**, 47
 Franks and, **40**
Cicero, 18
Circassians, 35
Cisalpine Gaul, **12**, *12*
Citizenship, Athenian, **3**, **4**, **7**
City-states, Etruscan, **10**, 11
Civilization,
 Greek, **5**
Clans,
 Japanese, **52**, *52*
Claudius, **18**, *18*
Cleopatra, **16**, *19*
Clothing,
 Aztec, **61**
 Greek, *8*
 Inca, **62**
 Maya, **56**
Clovis I, **40**, *40*
Codices, **59**
Coins, Chinese, **26**
Colonies,
 Etruscan, **10**
 Greek, *8*
Colosseum, **18**, *18*
Constantine, **24**, *25*
Constantinople, 24, **24**, *24*
Consuls, Roman, **18**
Coptic church, 24, *24*
Cordoba, **33**, 38
Corinth, **3**
Cortés, Hernando, 59
Criminals, Inca, **62**
Crusader knight, *37*
Crusades, **35**
 Saladin and, **38**
Culhua, **59**, *59*
Cynics, **4**

D
Dacia, **17**
Dagda, **12**
Dalriada, **42**, *42*
Damascus, **33**, 38-9
Dancing,
 Mayan, *57*
Danelaw, **42**, 43
Danes, 44–5
Darius III, **14**, *15*
Deities,
 Aztec, **60**, *60*
 Celtic, **12**, *12*
 Etruscan, **10-1**
 Roman, **18**
Delhi,
 Iron Pillar, **31**, *32*
 Sultanate of, **32**
Delian League, **4**
 Pelepponesian League and, **7**
Delos, *3*
Delphi, *3–4*
Demeter, *4*, *5*
Democracy, **5**
Democritus, **8**
Demosthenes, 14
Desmesne, **46**
Dhimmis, 35
Diamond Sutra, **28**
Diocletian, 19
Diogenes, **4**
Domesday Book, **46**
Draco, **5**, *5*
Drama,
 Greek, **5**, *5*
 Japanese, **52–3**, *53*
Druids, **12**
Dublin, **44**, *44*
Dutch traders, **52**

E
Eddas, **45**
Education,
 Franks and, **40**
Elba, *10*
Ellora caves, **30**, *30*
Emir, 36
Engineers,
 Etruscan, **10**
 Roman, *18*, *19*, *19*
England, **46**
English,
 Agriculture, **43**
 Gods, **43**, *43*
 Literature, **43**
 Map, *42*
Ennius, *19*

Ericsson, Leif, **44**, 45
Ethiopia(ns), 49
 Prester John and, **49**
Etruscans, 10–1
 Arts and crafts, **10**, 11, *11*
 City states, **10**, **11**
 Colonies, **10**
 Deities, **10**
 Engineering, **10**
 Map, *10*
 Society, 10, *10*
Euclid, **6**
Euripides, **5**, *5*
Europe, Feudal, 46–8
Ezana of Axum, 49

F
Fa-hsien, **31**
Fatima, 35–6
Fatimite, **36**, 38
Feudal, Europeans, 46–8
 Agriculture, **46**, 46–7, **48**
 Hunting, **47**
 Map, *46*
 Measurements, **47**
 Science, **48**
 Society, 46, **47–9**, 47–9
 Trade, **49**
 Warfare, **46**, 48
Fire,
 Greek, **25**
 Guns, **26**
France, **40**
Franks, 40–1
 Administration, **40**
 Architecture and art, **40**, *40*
 Church and, **40**
 Education and, **40**
 Map, *40*
 Monasteries and, **41**
Frederick Barbarossa, **47**
Freeholders, **46**, *46*, *47*
Fujiwara clan, **52**, *52*

G
Galatians, **12**
Galen, **21**
Galleys, Hellenistic and Carthaginian, *9*
Gaugamela, **15**
Gaul(s), **10**, *12*
 Cisalpine, **12**
 Transalpine, **13**
 Tribes, **12**
Genghiz Khan, **55**, *55*
Geography, Arab, 37
 Ptolemy and, *38*
Ger, **54**, *54–5*
Germanic tribes, 41
Germany, **44**, **47**
Ghana, **49**, *49*, **49**, 50
Gladiators, **19**, *19*
Glastonbury, **12**
Gobi Desert, **54**
Gods/Goddesses,
 Anglo-Saxon, **43**, *43*
 Celtic, *76*
 Viking, **45**
Government,
 Greek, **4**, **5**, **7**
 Roman, 18, *18*, 22
Gracchus, 19
Granada, **33**, **36**, *36*
Great Schism, 25
Greeks, 3–9
 Architecture, **3**, *3–5*, 5, *6*
 Civilization, **5**
 Colonization, **8**
 Drama, **5**, *5*
 Fire, **25**
 Government, **4**, **5**, **7**
 Language, **7**
 Law, **5**
 Mathematics, **6**
 Medicine, 6–7
 Peloponnesian Wars, **9**
 Philosophy, **4**, **5**, **8**, **9**
 Religion, **5**
 Science, **8**
 Ships, **9**
 Society, 3–4, *7*
Greenland, **44**, *44*
Gunpowder, **26**
Gupta dynasty, **30**, **31**
 Art, **31**
 Literature, 30–1
 Map, *30*

H
Hagia Sophia, 24–5
Hajj, **35**, **36**
Hallstatt, **12**, *13*
Hangchow, **26**, **27**
Hannibal, **20**, *20*
Harold II, **42**
Harsha, **31**
Harun al-Rashid, 36
Haruspicy, **10**
Hasan, **36**
Hausa states, **49**, 51
Hengist and Horsa, **42**
Hermes, **5**
Herodotus, **6**
Herophilus, **15**
Hesiod, **6**
Hideyoshi, Toyotomi, **53**
Hinduism, **94**

Hippocrates of Cos, **6–7**
Holy Roman Empire, **46**, **47**
Homer, 5
 Odyssey, *5*
Hoplites, **6**, *6*, *7*, *8*, **15**
Horace, 20
Horses,
 Mongol, **54**
Huitzilopochtli, 59
Hulagu, **39**, *39*, **54**
Huns, **17**
 White, **32**
Hunting,
 Alexander the Great and, *15*
 Feudal Europe, **47**
 Inca, **62**
 Mayan, **57**

I
Iberians, **36**
Ibn Batuta, **33**, 49–50
Iceland, **44**, *44*
Iconoclasts, **25**
Icons, **25**
Ieyasu, 53
Ife bronze, **49**, *49*, 51
Illyria(ns), **14**, *15*
Iman, **36**
Incas, 62–4
 Agriculture, **62**, 64, **64**
 Architecture, **62–3**, *63*
 Art, *63–4*
 Clothes, **62**
 Criminals, **62**
 Map, *62*
 Mummies, *63*
 Religion, 64
 Roads, **64**
 Sacrifice, *62*
 Society, 63, *63*, 64
Indians, Later, 30–2
 Art(s), *30-1*
 Architecture, 30–1
 Literature, 30–1
 Mathematics, **31**
Infantry, Macedonian, **15**
Innocent III, Pope, **47**
Iron,
 African, 50–1
Isfahan, **54**, **55**
Islam
 Muhammad and, 33
Issus, *79*
Itza rulers, **57**, 58

J
Jaguar cult, *63*
Janus, **18**
Japanese, 52–3
 Architecture, **53**
 Arts, **53**
 Literature, **53**
 Religion, **52–3**, *53*
 Tea ceremony, **53**
 Theatre, **52–3**, *53*
 Trade, **52–3**
Jayavarman II, **30**, 32
Jerusalem, *33*, **36**
Jesus of Nazareth, **20**
Jousting, **47**, *47*
Juno, **19**
Jupiter, **19**
Justinian I, **20**, 24, *24–5*
Jutes, **17**, 43

K
Kaaba, **33**, *35*
Kabuki, **52**
Kaifeng, **26**, *27*
Kairouan, **33**, 38
Kalidasa, **31**
Kama Sutra, 30–1
Kanem–Bornu, **49**, 51
Karakorum, **54**, **55**
Khmers, **32**
 Angkor and, **30**
Khwarizmi, 37
Kiev, *24*, **25**
Kilwa, **49**, *49*, **49**
Kin kingdom, **26**, **27**
Kola nuts, **50**
Kolumbi Saleh, **49**, 50
Koran, **34**
 Hajj and, **36**
Kuan-yin, **29**
Kublai Khan, **27**, 55, **55**
Kush, **49**, 50
Kwangchow (Canton), **26**
Kyoto, **52**

L
La Tène art, **12**
Lacedaemon, *3*
Language,
 Greek, **7**
 Latin, **20**
 Pictographic, **56**
Latin, **20**
La Venta, **56**, *56*
Law,
 Arab, **37**, 38
 Greek, **5**
 Roman, **20**
Leisure,
 Feudal Europe, **47**
Leo III, Pope, **41**, *41*

Li Po, **27**
Li Yuan, **27**
Library,
    Alexandria's, 16
Literature,
    Anglo-Saxon, 43
    Indian, 30-1
    Japanese, **53**
    Roman, 19
Livius, **20**
Livy, **20**
Longships, Viking, 44, **44**, 45
Lost wax process, 50, *50*
Loyang, *26*, **27**
Lucretius, **21**
Lug, 12

M
Macedonia(ns), 14-5, **16**
    Dynasty, **25**
    Infantry, **15**
    Map, *14*
    Phalanx, **15**
    Philip II and, 14
    See also Alexander the Great
Machu Picchu, 62-3, **63**
Maize, **57**
Malacca, **27**
Malawi, *49*, **50**
Mali, *49*, **50**, 50
Mamlukes, *36*, **37**
Manchus (Nuchen), **28**, 29
Mandaeans, **37**
Mandingo-Bambara, **50**
Mansa Musa, Emperor, **50**
Marco Polo, **28**, *29*, 55
Marcus Aurelius, **21**, *21*
Marius, **10**
    Sulla and, 11
Marrakesh, *33*, **37**, 39
Mars, **19**
Martel, Charles, 41
Massilia (Marseilles), *12*
Mathematics,
    Central American, **56**, 57
    Greek, **6**
    Indian, 31
Maya,
    Astronomy, **56**
    Ball game, **56**, *56-7*
    Calendars, **56**
    Hunters, **57**
    Mathematics, **56**
    Money (beans), **56**
    Pictographic language, **56**
    Priests, **58**
    Roads, **58**
    Sacrifices, **57**
Measurements,
    in Feudal Europe, **47**
Mecca, **33**, *33*
Medicine,
    Arab, *37*, **37**
    Greek, **6-7**
    Herophilus and, **15**
    Roman, **21**
Medina, **33**, *33*
Mehmet II, 25
Mercenaries,
    Hoplites and, **6**
Merovingians, 41
Metics, 7
Mexica tribe, *see* Aztecs
Mihrab, *34*, **37**
Minamoto shoguns, 52, **52**
Minerva, **19**
Ming dynasty, 27
    Porcelain, 27, **29**
Missionaries, Byzantine, 24
Mistletoe, **13**
Mitla, *56*, **57**
Mixtec, *59*, *60-1*
Monasteries, **41**, *41*
Money,
    Byzantine, **24**, *24*
    Cacao beans, **56**
    Chinese, **26**, 28
Mongols, *26*, **28-9**, 52, 54-5
    Arabs and, 39
    Architecture, 54, *54-5*
    Drama, **28**
    Kublai Khan and, 27
    Map, *54*
    Religion, **54**
    Society, 54
    Weapons, **54**, 55
Montezuma II, **60**
    Evil omens and, 60
Mosque architecture, **25**, 34, **34**, *36*
Mricchakatika, 30
Muawiya, Caliph, 34-5
Mughals, **31**
    Art, **55**
Muhammad, 33-4
Mummies, **63**
Music, African, 51
Muslims, *see* Arabs
Myths/Mythology,
    African, 51
    Aztec, **61**
    Icelandic, **44**
    Roman, *17*, **22**
    Viking, **45**

N
Nagasaki, *52*

Nero, **18**, 21, 22
No plays, **52**, *52*
Nok culture, **51**, *51*
Normans, **25**, 41
Norsemen, 41
Norwegians, 45
    See also Vikings
Novgorod, 45, **45**
Nuchen (Manchus), **28**, 29
Numidia, *33*
Numidians, 38

O
Oasis, *35*
Oaxaca, *59*, **60**
Obsidian, **57**
Octavian, 18, **21**
Odoacer, **21**
Odysseus, *5*
Offa's Dyke, 43
Old people, Inca, **63**
Oligarchy, **7**
Olmecs, 56-7
    Stone heads, **58**, *58*
Olympic Games, **7**
Oracles, 4, **7**
Origami, **53**
Orthodox church, Eastern, **24**
Osaka, 52
Ostrogoths, **21**
Ovid, **22**

P
Paper,
    Aztec books, **61**
Parakrama Bahu I, **31**
Parchment, **16**
Paris, **41**, *41*
Parthenon, **6**, *7*
Patriarchs, Eastern Orthodox, 24
Paul, Saint, **21**
Pax Romana, **22**
Peasants' War, **28**
Peloponnesian League/Wars, **7**, *9*
    Delian League and, **4**
Peking, *26*, **28**
Pepin the Short, 41
Pergamum, 12, *13*, 16
Pericles, 3, **7**
Perry, Commodore, **53**
Persepolis, **16**
Persians, **38**
    Peloponnesian Wars and, 9
Perusia, *10*
Phalanx, Macedonian, **15**
Philip II of Macedon, 14, **16**
    Court intrigues and, *14*
Philosophy,
    Greek, **4**, 5, **8-9**
Pictographs,
    Central Americans and, **57**
Picts, 42
Pisarro, Francisco, 64
Plato, *5*, 7, **8**
Politics, Roman, 18, **18**, **22**
Polo, Marco, **28**, *29*, 55
Pompeii, *17*, 22, **23**
Porcelain, Chinese, 27, **28**, **29**
Praetorian Guard, **22**
Prester John, **51**
Printing, block, **29**
Provincia, 12, **13**
Ptolemies, 16
    Alexandria and, 14, 16
    Cleopatra and, *16*
Ptolemy, **38**
Pythagoras, **6**

Q
Quetzacoatl, **58**
Quipu, *62*, **64**

R
Ramadan, **38**
Ravenna, *24*, **25**
Red,
    Turbans, **26**
Religion,
    Buddhism, **28**, **52-3**
    Christian, 21, 24, **35**, **37**, **42**, 43
    Greek, **5**
    Inca, **64**
    Islam, **33**
    Shamanist, **55**
    Shinto, **53**
Renaissance, **47**
Rhazes, **38**
Ritual bathing, *32*
Roads,
    Inca, **64**
    Mayan, **58**
    Roman, *18*
Romans, 17-23
    Architecture, 18-9, *19*, *23*
    Army, **20-1**
    Baths, *19*
    Christianity and, 21
    Consuls, **18**
    Engineering, **18**, 19, *19*
    Gladiators, **19**, *19*
    Latin and, **20**
    Law, 20
    Legends, *17*, **22**
    Literature, 19
    Map, *17*

Medicine, **21**
    Pax Romana and, **22**
    Politicians, 18, **18**, **22**
    Roads, *18*
    Trade, **19**, 20
Rome, *17*, 18-9, 24
    Colosseum, **18**, *18*
    Deities, **18**
    Punic Wars and, 22
    Western, **23**
Romulus, *17*, **22**
Roxane, Alexander and, *14*
Rozvi, **51**
Rus, 45

S
Sacrifice,
    Aztec, **59**, **60**
    Celtic, 12, **13**
    Human, **57**
    Inca, **62**
Sahara, *39*
Sailendra, **32**, *32*
Saladin, **38**
    Crusades and, *35*
Salat, **38**
Samarkand, **54**
Sampan, *26*
Saracen soldier, *37*
    Crusades and, *35*
Sassanians, **38**
Saum, **38**
Saxons, **17**, **43**
    Art, **43**
    Warrior, *43*
Science,
    Arab, 36
    Feudal European, **48**
    Greek, **8**
Scots, **43**
Seleucids, Seleucus and, 16
Seljuks, 39
Seneca, **22**
Serfs, 46, **47**, 48
Shamanists, **55**
Shankuntula, 31
    Kalidasa and, 31
Shi'ites, *35*, **39**
Shinto, **53**
Ships,
    Arab, **38**
    Chinese, **26**
    Greek, *9*
    Inca, **64**
    Viking, **44**, 45
Shogun, **53**
    Ashikaga, 52
    Minamoto, 52, **52**
Slav peoples, **25**
Slavery,
    Arab, **39**
    in Greece, **6-7**
    in Rome, 19
    Mayan, **57**, **58**
Society,
    Arab, **35**
    Celtic, 12, **13**
    Etruscan, **10**, *10*
    Feudal European, 46, **47**, *47*, 48, *48*
    Greek, **3-4**, 7
    Inca, **63-4**, **63**
Socrates, 5, **8**, *8*
Sogdiana, **16**
Soldier,
    Anglo-Saxon, **43**
    Crusader, *37*
    Greek hoplite, *8*
    Macedonian, *15*
    Roman, **20-1**
    Saracen, *37*
Solon, 5, **8**
Songhai, 51
Sophocles, **9**
South-East Asians, *see* Indians, Later
Spain,
    Islamic, 38
Spaniards, **61**, 64
Sparta, *3*, **9**
    Peloponnesian Wars and, 9
    Spartan Alliance and, **7**
Sri Lanka, **30**, *32*
Stoics, **9**
Stonehenge, **13**
Stupas,
    Borobudur, **30**, *30*, *32*
Suetonius, **22**
Sufis, **39**
Sui dynasty, **26**
Sulla, **11**
    Marius and, **10**
Sultanate of Delhi, **32**
Sundiata, **50**
Sung dynasty, 26-7
    Ceramics, 27, **29**, *29*
Sunnites, **39**
Surveying,
    Roman, *18*
Sutton Hoo, 43
Swahili, **51**
Swedes, 45
Syracuse, *3*, 8
Szechuan, *26*

T
Tacitus, **22**

Taghaza, **51**
Taira clan, 52
Tale of Genji, **53**
Tang dynasty, 26-7
    Art(s), 26-7, *29*
    Map, *26*
    Town planning, 27
Tarquinia, **11**
Tea ceremony, Japanese, *53*
Temples, Inca, **63**, 64
Tenochtitlan, **59**, **60**, **61**
Téotihuacan, *59*, **59**
Tepanecs, **60**, 61
Thais, **32**
Thebes,
    in Greece, *14*, **16**
Theodoric the Great, 21
Theodosius I, **21**
Theodosius II, 24
Thessalonica, 24
Thor, **45**, *45*
Thrace, **16**
Thucydides, **9**
Tiahuanaco, *62*, **64**
Tikal, **56**, *57*
Timur the Lame, **55**, *55*
Titicaca, Lake, *62*, **63**, *64*
Tlatelolco, **60**, 60, **61**
Toltecs, **57**, *58*
    Art, **58**
Tombouctou, *49*, 50
Town planning,
    Chinese, 27
Trade,
    African, **49**, 50, **51**
    Arab, **36**, **38**
    Chinese, **26**, 27-8
    Feudal European, **48**
    Japanese, **52-3**
    Roman, **19**, 20
Trajan, **22**, *22*
Transalpine Gaul, *12*, **13**
Trepanning, **64**, *64*
Tribes,
    Celtic, **12**
Tribune, Roman, 18, **22**
Trier, *24*, **25**
Tu Fu, **29**
Tuareg, **51**
Tughril, **39**
Tula, **59**, *59*
Turbans,
    Red, **26**
Turks, **25**, 39
Tyrrhenian Sea, *10*, **11**

U
Ujjain, **30**
Umar Khayyam, **39**
Umayyads, 34-5, **39**

V
Valens, **23**
Valentinian I, **23**
Vandals, **23**
Varangians, 45
Veii, *10*, **11**
Venerable Bede, **43**, *43*
Vezelay Abbey, *41*
Vikings, **41**, **43**, 44-5
    Longships, 44, **44**, 45
    Map, *44*
    Myths, **45**
    Warfare, 44
Villa, Roman, **23**
Vinland, **44**, **45**
Virgil, **23**
Visigoths, **23**
Volsinii, *10*
Voltumna, **11**

W
Wales, *42*, **43**
Walid, 35
Wall,
    Andean, **64**
Warfare,
    Feudal Europe, **46**, *48*
    Macedonian, **15**
    Roman, **20-1**
    Viking, 44
Weapons,
    Chinese gunpowder, **26**, 27
    Crusader, *37*
    Greek fire, **89**
    Macedonian, **15**
    Mongol, **54**, 55
    Roman, **20-1**
    Viking, **45**
Western Rome, **23**
White Huns, **32**
William the Conqueror, **43**, *43*

X
Xenophon, **9**

Y
Yang Chien, **26**, **29**
Yangchow, *26*
Yangtse Kiang, *26*, **29**
Yuan dynasty, **27**
    Kublai Khan and, 27, *27*

Z
Zakat, **39**
Zanzibar, *49*, **51**

Mathematics, **56**, 57
Zen, **53**
Zin, **51**, *51*

Acknowledgements

Contributing artists
Marion Appleton, Peter Archer, Charles Bannerman, Raymond Brown, Richard Coggan, Chris Forsey, Geoff Hunt, Ivan Lapper, Dennis Lascelles, Jim Marks, Nigel Osborne

The Publishers also wish to thank the following:
Ashmolean Museum, Oxford 42C
Bibliothèque Nationale, Paris 38TL
Bodleian Library, Oxford 45TR
Jean Bottin 4T, 61C
British Library 46C
British Museum 7TC, 47BR
Peter Clayton 6B
Colorpix 5TL, 32C, 59C
Douglas Dickins 13B, 15B, 30BR, 33B, 35B, 37B, 38B, 39B, 52B, 60B, 64B
Robert Estail 42B
Werner Forman Archive 3BR, 12B, 22B, 26B, 27BR, 29BR, 34BC, 34BR, 36B, 36TL, 44B, 45B, 50B, 53B, 55BR, 57B, 58B, 59B, 61B
Fotomas Index 47BC
Sonia Halliday 7BC, 17B, 22TL, 23B, 25TL CR, 40CR
Robert Harding Associates 3BC, 7BR, 9BR, 11BC BR, 27BC, 28B
Michael Holford 5TR, 10B, 18, 20B, 26C, 34CL, 35C, 36TL, 43CB, 48C, 49, 50TL, 51B, 53TL, 58TL, 59C, 63CR
Sarah King 39BR
Kunsthistorisches Museum, Vienna 13CR
William Macquitty 30BC, 38TR
Middle East Archive 35TR
Tony Morrison 62B, 63B
Oesterreichische Nationalbibliothek, Vienna 39C
Josephine Powell 18B, 19B, 21B, 24B, 25B, 31B, 32B, 49B
Walter Rawlings 63TR
Scala 46B
Servizio Editoriale Fotografico 11TR, 14CL
Ronald Sheridan 3, 4BR, 5TB, 6TR, 8B, 9BC, 10CL, 11CL, 14B, 16B, 17C, 19, 24C, 34CL, 36C, 40B, 41CR B, 56B
Snark International 41TL, 48TR B
Spink & Son Ltd 27TR
Mireille Vautier 52C, 57T, 64TC
ZEFA/Clive Sawyer 33C